Foreword

Your wedding day is a day
filled with beautiful memories
you'll cherish forever.

This book will help you create a look
all your own for that special day. With the
wide assortment of papers and embellishments
available, you'll be able to express your own personality
by making one-of-a-kind wedding invitations, favors, place
cards, programs, menu cards and much more.

You don't have to make everything yourself. You can easily mix and
match purchased items with do-it-yourself projects. You might want to
order your invitations from a printer, but then create your own place
cards, favors and thank you notes.

There's a section in the book called "10 Minute Invitations". These can be
made in a snap—especially if you have help from family and friends.

Enjoy this book and everything else that goes into creating a beautiful wedding.

Table of Contents

Supplies and Tools

A trip to your local craft or paper store will have you so inspired. There are so many beautiful papers, embellishments and tools to choose from. The following is a list of the supplies we used to create the projects in this book.

Paper

Bagasse - Handmade paper from India. Opaque, medium weight paper with natural fiber inclusions.

Cardstock – A stiff, heavyweight paper. Perfect base for cards.

Corrugated – Paper with a rippled surface. Available in a variety of colors including metallics.

Decorative printed paper – Used in card making, scrapbooking and other paper crafts. A huge selection of solids and prints are available.

Glassine – Thin, transparent paper. Envelopes of glassine are used to protect photos but are currently used as embellishments in card making and scrapbooking.

Kraft paper – An industrial paper resembling brown paper bags.

Japanese Origami paper – Brightly printed, lightweight japanese paper. Ordinarily used to make folded three-dimensional objects. Sold in packs with a wide variety of solid and print papers.

Mulberry paper – Made of fibers from the bark of a mulberry tree. Has a fibrous edge when torn.

Tissue paper - A thin, lightweight paper available in a wide variety of solids and prints.

Vellum – Translucent paper with a frosted appearance. Commonly used as an overlay.

Rubber stamps & ink pads

Rubber stamps – Thousands of designs available. Handy for making multiple images.

Dye ink pads – Pre-inked pads available in a large variety of colors. They're water based and quick drying and can be used for stamping on all types of paper.

Pigment ink pads – This ink is slow drying and best used with embossing powders. The sponges on the pads sit above the base of the container and can be used to ink directly to any size stamp rather than applying the stamp to the pad.

Embossing supplies

Embossing powders – Grainy material made of metal or plastic. When the powder is melted (with the use of a heat gun) it melts and adheres to the paper. Available in a wide range of colors.

Heat Gun – A hand-held implement used for embossing. Heat is applied directly to the stamped surface.

Note: A hair dryer is not hot enough for use with embossing powders.

Adhesives

Glue stick – lip balm-type container. Glue is rubbed to the surface of the paper. Provides a smooth, permanent bond. Look for acid-free.

Hot glue gun with glue sticks – Sticks are inserted into the gun. When the gun heats up, glue is dispensed when the trigger is pulled. Ideal for applying larger items such as bows, buttons and other embellishments. Not recommended for applying paper to paper because it tends to be lumpy and uneven. When using a glue gun with paper projects, a low melt gun works best.

Craft glue – Such as Tacky glue. Ideal for applying embellishments. It dries clear and is easy to clean up. It's slower drying than a glue gun.

Double-sided tape – Ideal for layering paper. Not as permanent as glue and tends to melt when heated. Some double-sided tapes are available in handy dispensers.

Cutting tools

Craft knife – Has angled blade on a cylindrical handle. Used for cutting details and clean lines.

Decorative scissors – Many different designs are available from deckle edges to scalloped and pinked. Creates beautiful edges on paper.

Punches

Decorative punches – Create interesting cut shapes and designs on paper.

Corner punches – Cuts a design on the edge or corner of the paper.

Hole punch – Cuts a hole in paper. Available in designs such as squares, hearts and even teddy bears. Punched out shapes can also be used as confetti or embellishments that can be glued to cards as decorative accents.

Stylus – An instrument with a ball point end used to score or to emboss paper.

Calligraphy pen – A pen with a broad nib that creates beautiful letters with thin and thick lines.

Other supplies that may be needed:

Sharp scissors
Paper cutter
Paint
Metal ruler
Computer and printer
Tracing paper
Transparent tape
Velcro® dots

The honour of your presence
Is requested at the marriage of
Amanda Lee Wallace
and
Eric Paul Smith
Saturday, the fourteenth of June
At two o'clock in the afternoon
At their home
406 Tumblecreek Lane
Fallbrook, California
immediately follow

You're Invited

Evoking the first day of spring, garden-fresh flowers typify this special season. As spirits soar, birds sing and breezes whisper, the wedding couple will begin their new life together as nature unfolds afresh. Our spring garden collection includes a vellum overlay on the green leaf decorated invitation, place card, save the date card, photo album, wedding planner notebook, shower invitation and vellum cone favor.

Save the Date

Patsy Neeley

Garden Wedding

Invitation

You'll need:
Ivory cardstock
Check paper, Tightweave green
  #61165 (Memories in the Making)
Green Leaf Spray vellum #61163
  (Memories in the Making)
12" ivory sheer ribbon, 1" wide
Glue stick
Glue gun
Font: Edwardian Script

1. Cut cardstock and green paper
$8\frac{1}{2}$" x 11". Glue them together.
Score and fold the card in half.

2. Print the wedding information on
ivory paper and cut $3\frac{1}{2}$" x $6\frac{1}{4}$".
Center and glue to the card.

3. Cut vellum $4\frac{1}{2}$" x $7\frac{1}{4}$". Center
over the invitation and glue along
the top edge only.

4. Tie the ivory ribbon into a bow
and hot glue it to the card.

Shower Invitation

You'll need:
Check paper, Tightweave green
  #61165 (Memories in the Making)
Green Leaf Spray vellum #61163
  (Memories in the Making)
Two Tone Stripe green paper
  #61175 (Memories in the Making)
Solid lime paper #61084 (Memories
  in the Making)
Ivory cardstock
Glue stick
Font: Edwardian Script

1. Cut green check paper and ivory
cardstock 4" x 5" and glue them
together.

2. Cut the green striped paper $2\frac{1}{2}$" x
5" and the leaf vellum $2\frac{3}{4}$" square.

3. Score, then fold the vellum
square in half on the diagonal to
form a triangle.

4. Cut across the triangle $\frac{1}{4}$" from
the fold on one side to form a flap.

5. Center the triangle on the stripe
paper with the fold on the top edge
and flap folded onto the back. Glue
the flap to the back of the card.

6. Glue the green stripe paper along
the sides and bottom of the check
card to form a pocket.

7. Print the "You're invited" information on the lime green paper.

8. Cut the paper 3" x 3" and insert
in the pocket with "You're invited"
extending above.

Save the Date

You'll need:
Check paper, Tightweave green
  #61165 (Memories in the Making)
Green Leaf Spray vellum #61163
  (Memories in the Making)
Two Tone Stripe green #61175
  (Memories in the Making)
Ivory cardstock
Glue stick
Font: Edwardian Script

1. Cut the green check and ivory
cardstock 5" x 7". Glue them
together. Score and fold in half.

2. Cut the stripe paper $2\frac{1}{2}$" x 4".
Center on the check card and glue
in place.

3. Print "Save the Date" on the leaf
vellum paper using your computer
or a stamp. Cut 2" x $3\frac{1}{4}$", then glue
in the center of the green stripe
card.

4. Write the name of the couple,
wedding date, time and place on the
inside of the card.

Note
Refer to page 80 before beginning your invitation projects for
sample wording.

Wedding Album

You'll need:
Purchased album with laced ribbon
  8" x 9"
Check paper, Tightweave green
  #61165 (Memories in the
  Making)
Green Leaf Spray vellum #61163
  (Memories in the Making)
Green floral #AG003 (Anna Griffin)
Ivory cardstock
Oval cut-out (Anna Griffin)
Photograph
Glue stick

1. Cut the green check paper $7\frac{3}{4}$" x
11". Glue to the album front. Wrap
around to the inside of the cover
and glue. (See page 23 for further
instructions).

2. Cut a strip of green floral paper
$2\frac{1}{2}$" x 12". Position on the center of
the green check paper. Fold to the
inside cover of the album. Glue in
place.

3. Cut a piece of ivory cardstock 6"
x 7" and leaf vellum $5\frac{1}{4}$" x $6\frac{1}{4}$".

4. Glue the photograph to the back
of the oval cut-out. Layer the paper,
photograph and oval cut-out on the
album cover. Use a glue stick to
glue in place.

Place Card

You'll need:
Two Tone Stripe green paper
  #61175 (Memories in the Making)
Green Leaf Spray vellum #61163
  (Memories in the Making)
Ivory cardstock
Ivory paper
Calligraphy pen
Glue stick

1. Cut the green stripe paper and
cardstock 4" x 4" and glue them
together. Score, then fold in half.

2. Cut the leaf vellum $1\frac{1}{2}$" x $3\frac{1}{4}$". Glue in the center of the green stripe card.

3. Cut ivory paper $\frac{1}{2}$" x $2\frac{1}{2}$". Glue in the center of the vellum.

4. Write the guest's name on the card using a calligraphy pen.

Wedding Planner

You'll need:
Purchased journal 5" x $6\frac{1}{2}$"
Ivory paper
Lt. green solid paper
Dark green solid paper
Green floral vellum #AG003
  (Anna Griffin)
Scallop edge scissors
Glue stick
Double-sided tape
Adhesive embellishment, Leaf Heart
  #66544 (Memories in the Making)

1. Cut the light green paper 6" x 8".

2. Starting $\frac{3}{4}$" from the spiral binding, use a glue stick to affix the paper to the album.

3. Wrap the top, bottom and side to the inside cover and glue in place. (See page 23 for finishing corners).

4. Cut ivory paper 2" x 8". Glue to the center of the green paper. Wrap ends to the inside cover and glue in place.

5. Cut vellum $4\frac{1}{2}$" x 5". Use a scallop edge scissors to cut one 5" edge. Place double-sided tape along the right, left and bottom edges of the vellum. Affix this piece at the bottom of the green paper forming a pocket. Wrap the right side of the vellum to the inside cover and press in place. Use this pocket to hold business cards from caterers, florists, etc.

6. Cut a piece of dark green paper $1\frac{1}{2}$" square. Adhere to the ivory paper using a glue stick.

7. Attach the adhesive embellishment.

Bubbles

You'll need:
Bottle of bubbles
Decorative stickers, green #AG614
  (Anna Griffin)

1. Following the photograph, attach the stickers to the bottle of bubbles.

Cone Favor

You'll need:
Green Leaf Spray vellum #61163
  (Memories in the Making)
White tulle
12" green ribbon, $\frac{1}{4}$" wide
Jordan almonds, green and white
Scallop edge scissors
Double-sided tape

1. Trace and cut out the pattern on page 78.
2. Place the pattern on the leaf vellum and cut out. Use the scallop edge scissors where indicated.
3. Form into a cone overlapping the edges about $\frac{1}{2}$". Use double-sided tape to hold edges in place.
4. Cut a piece of tulle into a 10" square. Lay flat and place candied almonds in the center. Gather up the sides and tie with a ribbon at the top.
5. Insert the candy in the cone. Place beside the plates at the reception.

Tip
Purchase envelopes first for any projects you'll be making. Then measure and cut your paper to fit the envelopes you've chosen.

"Save the date" cards are sent when a number of guests live out of town or out of the country. The cards are sent at least three months prior to the wedding so that all necessary travel plans can be made.

Also send "save the date" cards when the wedding will be held in a resort area for guests who might want to plan a vacation around the wedding.

Sample card:

Please save the date of
Saturday, the tenth of June
for the wedding of
Miss Jane Anne Smith
to
Mr. Robert Alton White

Mrs. and Mrs. Allen Jay Smith
Invitation to follow

Magnetic sheets with adhesive backing can be used to make Save the Date cards. The guests can then display it on their refrigerator. You can find magnetic sheets in craft stores. Follow the manufacturer's instructions for printing or stamping on the sheets.

Or as an alternative, a small magnet can be applied to the back of the card which also can be easily displayed.

Lavender Mist

An English garden of lilacs, hydrangeas, violets or lavender could all be the flowers of choice to coordinate with this Lavender Mist selection. A joyous mixture of checks, stripes and vellum combine to create the invitation, guest book, shower invitation, place card, save the date card and favor.

Save the Date

The honour of your presence
Is requested at the marriage of

Courtney Anne Bradley
and
Chas Jason Clements

Saturday, the Fifteenth of July
At seven o'clock in the evening

The Willows
2955 Mission Road
Phoenix, Arizona

Reception immediately follows

Chas and Courtney
July 15, 2005

Lavender Mist

Invitation

You'll need:
White cardstock
White paper
Lavender mulberry paper
Lavender check paper,
   Window Screen #61167
   (Memories in the Making)
Stripe paper, Oxfordchalk Slate
   #6l059 (Memories in the Making)
Purple vellum #61068 (Memories
   in the Making)
12" sheer lavender ribbon, 1½" wide
Glue stick
Glue gun
Font: Curlz

1. Cut white cardstock 7½" x 10".
Score and fold in half.

2. Cut check paper 4½" x 7", mulberry paper, 4" x 6½".

3. Cut 1" squares of check, stripe and vellum.

4. Print invitation on white paper and cut to 3½" x 5".

5. Layer these papers referring to the photograph. Note that the small squares are placed on the diagonal.

6. Tie ribbon into a bow and hot glue to the upper portion of the card.

Place Card

You'll need:
White cardstock
Stripe paper, Oxfordchalk Slate
   #6l059 (Memories in the Making)
Lavender check paper, Window
   Screen #61167 (Memories in the
   Making)
Purple vellum #61068 (Memories
   in the Making)
Other
Font: Curlz

1. Cut cardstock and the stripe

paper 4½" square. Glue the stripe paper to the cardstock.

2. Score and fold the card in half.

3. Print guest's names on vellum leaving at least 1" between each name.

4. Cut the check, lavender and cardstock into 1½" squares.

5. Position the vellum paper with the name over the 1½" cardstock square with the square on the diagonal and the name running across the middle. Turn over and trace around the shape lightly with a pencil. Cut out the vellum and glue to the cardstock.

6. Glue these three squares on the diagonal and overlapping to the folded card (see photograph).

Favor

You'll need:
Purchased small white box with
   handles, 3" x 3"
Lavender check paper,
   Window Screen #61167
   (Memories in the Making)
Stripe paper, Oxfordchalk Slate
   #6l059 (Memories in the Making)
Purple vellum #61068 (Memories
   in the Making)
Lavender shred
White tulle
12" lavender ribbon, 1½" wide
Scallop edge scissors
Jordan almonds, white and lavender
Font: Curlz

1. Cut around the top edge of the box using scallop edge scissors, cutting off the handle.

2. Cut a strip of the striped paper ½" x 10" and glue around the box.

3. Print name of bride and groom and date of wedding on the vellum paper. See step 5 of "Place Card" for centering. Cut into 1¼" squares.

4. Cut check paper 1¾" square. Glue the vellum piece to this piece and then glue on the diagonal to the front of the box.

5. Cut a 12" square of tulle. Place candied almonds in the center. Gather up and wrap with the lavender ribbon and tie into a bow.

6. Fill the box with lavender shred. Place the tulle bag in the shred.

Thank You Note

You'll need:
Lavender check paper,
   Window Screen #61167
   (Memories in the Making)
Stripe paper, Oxfordchalk Slate
   #6l059 (Memories in the Making)
Lavender stripe #AG143
   (Anna Griffin)
Purple vellum #61068 (Memories
   in the Making)
Craft glue
Font: Curlz

1. Cut cardstock and check paper into 5" x 7" pieces. Glue the check paper to the cardstock. Score and fold up one end 2" and the top edge down 1¾".

2. Print "Many" and "Thanks" on the vellum paper. Cut them into 1" squares with the words on the diagonal (see step 5 "Place Card" for centering).

3. Cut 1½" squares of each stripe paper and glue the vellum squares to each striped square (refer to photo).

4. Glue these two squares to the top edge of the flap of the card.

5. After writing the thank you note, fold the top down.

Guest Book

You'll need:

Purchased journal 6" x 7"
Lavender mulberry paper
Lavender check paper,
  Window Screen #61167
  (Memories in the Making)
Stripe paper, Oxfordchalk Slate
  #6l059 (Memories in the Making)
Lavender stripe #AG143 (Anna
  Griffin)
Purple vellum #61068 (Memories
  in the Making)
12" sheer lavender ribbon, 1½" wide
Glue gun
Glue stick
Font: Curlz

1. Cut mulberry paper 7½" x 8" and glue to the cover of the album, wrapping the edges to the inside of the cover and gluing. (See page 23 for finishing corners.)

2. Print "Guests" on the vellum paper and cut into 1½" square. (See step 5 "Place Cards" for centering.)

3. Cut the check and two stripe papers into 1½" squares. Glue the printed vellum to the lavender stripe square. Glue all three of the squares to the front of the album (refer to photo for placement).

4. Tie the ribbon into a bow and hot glue to the album as pictured.

Save the Date

You'll need:

Purchased white notecard 3½" x 5"
Purple vellum #61068 (Memories
  in the Making)
Stripe paper, Oxfordchalk Slate
  #6l059 (Memories in the Making)
Lavender check, Windowscreen
  #61167 (Memories in the Making)
6" white satin edged sheer ribbon,
  ½" wide
Hole punch

Scallop edge scissors
Glue stick
Font: Curlz

1. Use the computer, a rubber stamp or handwriting for "Save the Date" (or see page 35 for type you can copy and use) on the vellum paper. Cut 2½" x 5". Cut the bottom edge using a scallop edge scissors.

2. Use the computer (or rubber stamp) to create the date, time, and place information. Cut to 2½" x 4" and glue to the inside of the card.

3. Cut stripe paper 1" x 5", and the check paper 5" x 6½".

4. With a glue stick, adhere the stripe paper to the bottom portion of the notecard. Then glue the check paper to the card, starting ½" from the bottom edge and onto the back. Place the vellum ½" from the check paper and adhere with glue just along the fold.

5. Punch two holes in the top center front of the card and thread the ribbon through the holes from the front of the card to the back (A).

6. Cross the ribbons in the back and feed back through to the front (B).

7. Pull the ends taut and trim (C).

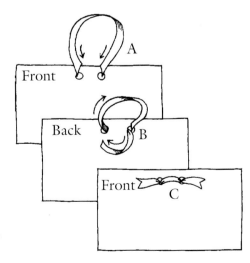

To create wedding accessories on your own computer and printer:

1. Open your word processing program.

2. Go to File
Page Set Up
Paper size

(Enter the paper size you'll be using.)

Click O.K.

3. Type the invitation information in the document window after selecting your font and type size.

4. Go to File

Print Preview.

(Is everything correct — spelling, spacing, etc.
If not, go back to the document and make any corrections or adjustments.)

5. Use a piece of scrap paper the same size as your invitation to print a test sheet to make sure the placement of the message is correct.

Make any adjustments.

6. Print invitations.

When printing multiple items on a page such as guest's names, "You're invited" etc, check the project instructions for the size of the finished item. Make sure you leave enough space between your typed information to make the correct cut.

Note: Use the manual feed on your printer for best results.

When printing on vellum, use a laser printer.

Patricia and Matthew
June 15, 2004

We look forward to
Celebrating with you
Please reply by October 18, 2004

Name _____ will attend
_____ not able to attend

Summertime breezes, days of sunshine and tranquility are symbols of a seaside wedding. The palest shades of blue and peach, fragile shells, and gossamer ribbons embellish these projects.

Mike McKinzie

Shown here, a shell-bedecked invitation, candle, place card, guest book and bubbles. The reply card and personalized chocolate bar favor round out this themed collection.

The honour of your presence
Is requested at the marriage of

Patricia Ann Cummins
and
Matthew Alan Scott

Saturday, the Sixteenth of June
At six o'clock in the evening

Wilshire Presbyterian Church
3600 Wilshire Boulevard
Los Angeles, California

Reception immediately follows

Patricia and Matthew
June 15, 2004

By the Sea

Wedding Invitation

You'll need:
Ivory cardstock
White vellum
Stamp: Shell Border #2674F
  (Posh Impressions)
Ink pads: blue, peach, pink, green
8" pink organza ribbon, $1\frac{1}{2}$" wide
Double-sided adhesive spacer
Glitter
Glue stick
Glue gun
Font: Edwardian Script

1. Cut ivory cardstock 7" x 10". Score and fold in half. Stamp over the front of the card with the shell border stamp and assorted inks.

2. Print the invitation on the vellum paper and cut 5" x 7". Place the vellum on top of the stamped card and glue along the top edge using a glue stick.

3. Tie the ribbon in a knot and glue on the top of the card using a glue gun.

4. To make the individual shells, stamp ivory cardstock using the shell border stamp and desired color of ink (you'll need more shells for the following projects). Cut around the shell leaving a slight border using a craft knife. Rub a glue stick on the shell where you would like to highlight with glitter. Dust with glitter and shake off the excess.

5. Use small double-sided adhesive spacer to attach the shells to the ribbon.

Place Card

You'll need:
Ivory cardstock
Green Floral paper #AG003
  (Anna Griffin)
Purple Marble paper #61224
  (Memories in the Making)
Ivory paper
Stamp: Shell #2674F
  (Posh Impressions)
Ink pad: peach
Glitter
Deckle edge scissors

1. Cut ivory cardstock 4" x 4". Score and fold in half.

2. Print guests' names on ivory paper (be sure to allow enough space between names). Cut the paper 1" x $2\frac{3}{4}$" using the deckle edge scissors.

3. Cut the green floral paper $1\frac{1}{2}$" x $3\frac{1}{2}$" and the Marble paper $1\frac{1}{4}$" x $3\frac{1}{4}$".

4. Triple layer these papers to the place card.

5. Use a shell made previously (see step #4 of Wedding Invitation). Glue the shell to the place card.

Reply Card

You'll need:
Ivory cardstock
Purple Marble paper #61224
  (Memories in the Making)
Glitter
Font: Edwardian Script

1. Print the message on ivory cardstock. Cut 2" x $3\frac{1}{4}$" using deckle edge scissors. Glue this to a $2\frac{1}{4}$" x $3\frac{1}{2}$" piece of the marble paper.

2. Cut another piece of ivory cardstock 3" x $4\frac{1}{2}$" with the deckle edge

scissors and glue the double layer to the center of this card.

3. Apply the glue stick around the edge of the marble paper and dust with glitter. Shake off excess glitter.

Candle
(Favor or table decoration)

You'll need:
Frosted glass votive
Ivory paper
Stamp: Shell #2674F
  (Posh Impressions)
Ink pad: green
16" pink sheer ribbon, $1\frac{1}{2}$" wide
Glitter
Double-sided adhesive spacer

1. Wrap the ribbon around the glass votive and tie in a knot on the front. Notch the tails of the ribbon.

1. Use a shell made previously (see step 4 Wedding Invitation). Attach the shell to the knot of the ribbon using the adhesive spacer.

Chocolate Bar Favor

You'll need:
$5\frac{1}{2}$" chocolate bar with metallic
  wrapper
Ivory cardstock
Green floral #AG003 (Anna Griffin)
Pink floral #AG013 (Anna Griffin)
Ivory paper
Stamp: Shell #2674F (Posh
  Impressions for Rubber Stampede)
Ink pads: peach, green, blue
Deckle edge scissors

1. Print name of bride and groom and date of wedding on ivory card-

stock. Cut to 1" x 2¼" using deckle edge scissors.

2. Cut a piece of ivory cardstock 5" x 6". Stamp all over with the shell design using peach, green and blue ink. Wrap this around the candy bar overlapping edges on the back and glue.

3. Cut a piece of the green floral paper 1½" x 3" using deckle edge scissors. Cut the pink paper 1¼" x 2¾" using regular scissors. Layer these pieces along with the printed piece and glue to the candy bar (refer to photo).

Honeymoon Photo Album

You'll need:
Purchased ivory album 6" x 8"
Purple Marble paper #61224
  (Memories in the Making)
Green floral #AG003 (Anna Griffin)
Pink floral #AG013 (Anna Griffin)
White vellum
Ivory cardstock
Stamp: Shell #2674F
  (Posh Impressions)
Ink pads: blue, green, peach
Deckle edge scissors
Glitter
Double-sided adhesive spacers

1. Cut marble paper 7" x 8". With a glue stick, glue to the front of the album allowing for a 1½" border on the left side. Wrap the paper around to the inside cover and glue. (See page 23 for finishing corners).

2. Cut white vellum 2" x 8". Tear the edge of one long side to get a "wave" effect. Adhere the vellum to the bottom edge of the album. Rub the glue stick along the wavy edge of the vellum and dust with glitter.

3. Use deckle edge scissors to cut the green floral paper 2" x 3¾" and regular scissors to cut the pink floral paper 1½" x 3¼".

4. Print name of bride and groom and wedding date on ivory card stock. Cut into 1" x 2¾" strips using the deckle edge scissors.

5. Triple layer the pieces as shown in the photo and adhere to the front of the album.

6. Adhere shells previously prepared (see step 4, Wedding Invitation) along the left edge using the adhesive spacers.

Bubbles

You'll need:
Bottle of bubbles
White tulle
6" pink sheer ribbon, 1½" wide
Small pink shell
Glue gun

1. Cut the tulle into an 8" square. Place the bottle in the center and gather up the sides. Wrap ribbon around and tie into a bow. Trim the tulle if necessary.

2. Hot glue the shell to the front of the bow.

Make It Faster

To make a faster version of the Honeymoon Photo Album, omit step 2. The album will be just as beautiful, but will be made in half the time.

---

1. Practice your stamping technique on a piece of scrap paper before you begin.

2. The stamp pad should be clean and inked before using. If the pad is dry, a re-inker can be used. Add the ink a few drops at a time working it into the pad until the ink is even.

3. Lightly tap the stamp on the pad a few times. Check to make sure all areas of the design are inked. Stamp on scrap paper to test the image by holding the stamp firmly, pressing down. Press all around the top of the stamp to get a complete image.

4. Remove the stamp straight up, very carefully.

5. If the stamp is large, it helps to ink directly to the stamp using a small ink pad such as a cat's eye pigment brush pad from Color Box. You can "paint" your stamp with different colors using the cat's eye stamp pads to achieve some really unusual effects.

Try experimenting with these different stamping techniques for best results.

6. When you're finished stamping, clean the stamp using a stamp cleaner. There are several varieties on the market. Follow the manufacturer's instructions.

Red Toile

The sophistication of red toile and Victorian flowers are joined together to create this lovely union of wedding essentials. The invitation fits in a clever pocket, the matching items include a VCR cover, pop-up thank you note, place card and decorated candle.

Patricia and Matthew
June 15, 2004

Steve Brown

Patricia and Matthew
June 15, 2004

The honour of your presence
Is requested at the marriage of

Amanda Lee Wallace
and
Eric Paul Smith

Saturday, the fourteenth of June
At two o'clock in the afternoon

Red Toile

Place Card

You'll need:
Red floral paper #AG050
  (Anna Griffin)
Red toile paper #AG096
  (Anna Griffin)
Ivory cardstock
Glue stick

1. Cut the ivory cardstock and red floral paper 4" x 6". Glue together.
2. Score, then fold in half.
3. Cut a strip of toile paper $1\frac{1}{4}$" x 4". Glue the sides and bottom of the strip to the place card at the bottom edge.
4. Cut a piece of ivory cardstock 2" x $2\frac{1}{2}$". Print the name of the guest toward the top edge of the card. Slide the card into the toile pocket.

Wedding Video Cover

You'll need:
Red floral paper #AG115
  (Anna Griffin)
Red toile paper #AG096
  (Anna Griffin)
Ivory cardstock
Video cover
Glue stick
Font: Edwardian Script

1. Lay a piece of red floral paper on a flat surface with the wrong side up.
2. Open up the VHS cover and lay on the paper. Trace around it and cut paper slightly smaller. The finished size of this cover is $8\frac{3}{4}$" x $11\frac{3}{4}$".

3. Cut two strips of toile paper $1\frac{1}{4}$" x $11\frac{3}{4}$".
4. Print the names of the bride and groom and the wedding date on ivory paper. Cut a strip 1" x $11\frac{3}{4}$".
5. Center the strips on the floral paper (see photograph). Glue in place using a glue stick.
6. VHS covers usually have plastic over the cover with an opening at the top. This allows you to slide the decorated paper between the cover and the plastic.

Invitation

You'll need:
Burgundy floral paper #AG002
  (Anna Griffin)
Red toile paper #AG096
  (Anna Griffin)
Ivory paper
14" red ribbon, 1" wide
Glue stick
Glue gun
Font: Edwardian Script

1. Print the invitation on the ivory paper. Cut to 4" x 6".
2. Cut the burgundy floral paper to $5\frac{1}{2}$" x 8" and the toile, $3\frac{1}{2}$" x $5\frac{1}{2}$". Make a pocket by gluing the toile paper to the bottom portion of the floral paper. Glue just around the edges of three sides of the toile paper.
3. Slip the invitation into the pocket.
4. Tie a bow using the red ribbon and hot glue it to the top of the invitation.

Candle

You'll need:
Red toile paper #AG096
  (Anna Griffin)
Burgundy floral paper #AG002
  (Anna Griffin)
Ivory paper
3" pillar candle
Glue stick
Font: Edwardian Script

1. Print the bride and groom's name and the date of the wedding on ivory paper. Cut into a 1" x $2\frac{1}{4}$" strip.
2. Cut the burgundy paper $1\frac{1}{4}$" x $2\frac{3}{4}$".
3. Cut the toile paper 2" x 10". Glue the ivory strip to the center of the burgundy strip, then to the center of the toile strip.
4. Wrap this piece around the candle overlapping and gluing in the back to secure.

Tip

If you're having a DVD made of your wedding, you'll want to create a CD cover instead of the video cover using the same toile papers included in this collection. See pages 48 and 77 for CD cover instructions. You can create your own labels for the CD or have them custom made. See the internet site at www.weddingcd.cdbyme.com

Thank You Note

You'll need:
Red floral paper #AG115
  (Anna Griffin)
Red toile paper #AG096
  (Anna Griffin)
Ivory cardstock

1. Cut the red floral paper and the toile paper 3" x 6".

2. Measure in $1\frac{1}{2}$" from each short end and score. Fold ends to meet at center.

3. Open up the toile paper and lay flat, wrong side up (1). Open up the floral paper and lay wrong side up, across the center of the toile paper (2).

4. Cut a piece of ivory cardstock 3" x 3". Write the thank you message on the card and place in the center of the folded card.

5. Following the diagram, fold flap A to center (3). Fold flap B to center (4), then flap C to center (5). Fold D to center and tuck the right corner under the right bottom corner of flap A (6). See diagram.

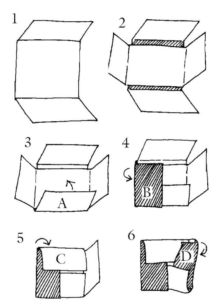

Thank you

Thank you

Thank you

Many thanks

(May be reproduced for personal use)

When planning your wedding budget, here's a list of items to include and suggested percentages:

• 2% Invitations, reply cards, save the date cards, programs, menu cards, place cards, favors, postage

• 4% Flowers for the church, reception, and for the wedding party

• 5% Music

• 6% Bride's attire, tuxedos

• 8% Clergy fees, rehearsal party, attendant gifts, limos

• 9% photography, videography

• 14% Engagement and wedding rings

• 14% Honeymoon

• 38% Reception

Whether you're paying the bills or your parents are, it's a good idea to sit down with everyone involved and find out how much each person is committing to the cost. You'll then be able to set a realistic budget and can start making all the necessary decisions.

It's helpful to set up a separate bank account specifically for wedding costs.

Black Toile

Black and white provides a stylish theme for an elegant wedding. The introduction of gold and bright pink lends freshness to this winning combination. The elegant, yet simple invitation is seen here with a place card, photo album, card box and a decorated package of incense as the wedding favor.

Megan and Alex
June 15, 2004

The honour of your presence
Is requested at the marriage of

Megan Tosca Hill
and
Alex John Myers

Saturday, the Ninth of September
At seven o'clock in the evening

Wavecrest
233 Highway 101
Del Mar, California

Reception immediately follows

Cards

Patricia

Megan and Alex
June 15, 2004

Invitation

You'll need:
Kraft cardstock
Gold foil
Black/gold paper #AG034
   (Anna Griffin)
Ivory paper
4" gold metallic ribbon, $\frac{1}{2}$" wide
Glue gun
Glue stick
Font: Papyrus

1. Print invitation information on ivory paper and cut to 3" x 5".
2. Cut the black/gold paper $3\frac{3}{4}$" x $5\frac{3}{4}$", the gold foil 4" x 6".
3. Cut the kraft cardstock 7" x 10". Score and fold in half.
4. Layer and glue the paper as pictured in the photograph.
5. Tie the gold ribbon in a knot and and hot glue to the top center of the ivory paper.

Place Card

You'll need:
Gold corrugated paper
Black toile paper #AG061
   (Anna Griffin)
Ivory paper
Fancy edge scissors
Glue stick
Font: Papyrus

1. Print the guests' names on ivory paper and cut into $\frac{1}{2}$" x 1" (or to the length of the name).
2. Cut the gold corrugated paper 4" square. Score and fold in half.
3. Cut the the toile paper $1\frac{1}{2}$" x $3\frac{1}{2}$" using fancy edge scissors.
4. Glue the name strip to the toile paper and the toile paper to the gold card.

Photo Album

You'll need:
Purchased album 5" x $6\frac{1}{2}$"
Black toile paper #AG061
   (Anna Griffin)
Gold foil
Black/gold paper #AG034
   (Anna Griffin)
Corrugated paper
Ivory paper
Font: Papyrus

1. Print the couple's name and the wedding date on the ivory paper and cut 1" x 2".
2. Cut the corrugated 2" x 3", the black/gold paper 3" x 4" and the gold foil $3\frac{1}{4}$" x $4\frac{1}{4}$".
3. Cut the black toile paper 4" x 8" and cover the album. (see instructions page 23).
4. Layer and glue the cut pieces to the top front of the album.

Favor ~ Incense

You'll need:
Package of incense
Black/gold paper #AG034
   (Anna Griffin)
Corrugated heart die cut (Paper Reflections)
Bright pink cardstock
Ivory paper
12" bright pink silk ribbon, $\frac{1}{8}$" wide
Pinking shears
Font: Papyrus

1. Print the couple's name and date of wedding on ivory paper. Cut to 1" x 2".
2. Cut the bright pink cardstock $1\frac{1}{2}$" x $2\frac{3}{4}$" using pinking shears (for paper).
3. Glue the name piece to the pink paper and glue to the bottom portion of the incense package.
4. Cut the black/gold paper $6\frac{1}{2}$" x $6\frac{1}{2}$" using the pinking shears. Wrap this piece around the incense package and overlap at the back. Either glue or use double-sided tape to secure.
5. Punch two holes in the top portion of the die-cut heart. Thread the ribbon through the holes from the back and tie in the front. Trim the tails. Glue to the black/gold paper as pictured. (If you can't find the corrugated die-cut heart, a pattern is provided on page 59.)

Card Box

You'll need:
Brown and black striped hat box
Gold paper
Black/gold paper #AG034
   (Anna Griffin)
Glue stick
Font: Papyrus

1. Print "Cards" on gold paper and cut $1\frac{3}{4}$" x $3\frac{1}{2}$".
2. Cut the black and gold paper $2\frac{1}{2}$" x $4\frac{1}{2}$". Glue the gold piece on the black/gold piece and then glue to the side of the box.

More Ideas

To make table number cards: cut a piece of the gold corrugated about 7" x 10" and fold in half. Create numbers either by computer or with a stencil on ivory paper. Cut the ivory paper a bit smaller than the corrugated and glue to the center using a glue stick. Place the folded number card in the center of the table.

Covering a photo album:

1. Place opened album on the wrong side of the paper. Trace around the album with a pencil. Add one inch all the way around and cut, angling the corners.
At the bottom end of the spine of the album, cut two slits in the paper at each edge of the spine.

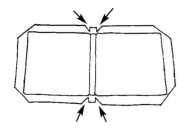

2. Lay the paper wrong side up with album on top. Apply a thin layer of glue to all the edges of the paper. Pull the paper carefully up and onto the album cover.

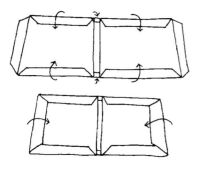

3. Cut another piece of paper for the inside front and inside back of the album. Glue in position to neatly finish off the inside.

Cards

cards

Cards

Cards

Cards

(May be reproduced for personal use)

This is the box in which guests can place cards and monetary gifts. Display the card box on a table near the guest book or near the area where the other gifts are placed.

The box can be used after the wedding to keep mementos of the special day.

Other types of boxes to use:

1. Papier mache boxes are available in many shapes and sizes that will lend themselves to card boxes. You might choose a square, round or a heart-shaped box.

2. A large square white gift box would work well. Decorate it with ribbons, bows and silk flowers in the colors of the wedding.

3. A shoe box can be covered with decorative paper with a slit cut in the top.

4. Visit your local import store for box ideas. Many have interesting boxes from the orient that have the look of treasure chests.

5. A small vintage cosmetic case that has been decoupaged with floral paper would work well as a card box. Just keep the top open and display the "card" strip on the inside top.

6. A vintage wooden file drawer could serve as a card box. Display "cards" in the little slide-in area on the front of the drawer.

7. Have your florist save some extra flowers from the the centerpieces. Use the flowers to decorate the card box.

Blue Elegance

Guests

Thank You

Blue symbolizes purity, fidelity and love. What better color choice for a wedding. These soft blue accessories feature gorgeous floral papers and gossamer ribbons. Included on this page—an invitation, decorated votive candle holder, guest book, wedding program and thank you card.

The honour of your presence
Is requested at the marriage of

Amanda Lee Wallace
and
Eric Paul Smith

Saturday, the fourteenth of June
At two o'clock in the afternoon

At their home
1406 Tumblecreek Lane
Fallbrook, California

Program

In love the paradox occurs that two beings become
one and yet remain two.
— Eric Fromm

Invitation

You'll need:
Ivory cardstock
Dark blue floral paper #AG178
  (Anna Griffin)
Light blue floral paper #AG045
  (Anna Griffin)
Blue solid paper
24" white sheer wire edged ribbon,
  $1\frac{1}{2}$" wide
Font: Apple Chancery

1. Cut the ivory cardstock 7" x 10". Score and fold in half.

2. Cut the light blue floral 2" x 7" and the other blue floral 3" x 7".

3. Print the invitation in the middle of the solid blue paper and trim to $3\frac{1}{2}$" x $5\frac{1}{2}$".

4. Using a glue stick, adhere the dark blue floral paper first and then the light blue over the top on the left edge of the card.

5. Adhere the invitation paper over the top of the first two paper strips centering on the folded cardstock. Leave slightly more space at the bottom than the top.

6. Wrap the ribbon around the front section of the invitation and tie in a knot on the front. Cut the ends on an angle and pinch each end in loose fan-folds.

Candle

You'll need:
Frosted glass votive holder
Patterned white vellum
16" blue sheer ribbon, 2" wide
Craft glue

1. Cut the vellum 2" x 8", wrap around the votive holder and adhere in the back.

2. Wrap the sheer blue ribbon over the vellum and glue at the back.

3. Fold the ribbon in half lengthwise and tie around the holder. Make a pretty bow and trim the tails.

Thank You Note

You'll need:
Purchased embossed note cards
Blue solid paper
Light blue floral paper #AG045
  (Anna Griffin)
Dark blue floral paper #AG148
  (Anna Griffin)
Ivory paper
Glue stick
Font: Apple Chancery

1. Print "Thank You" several times on ivory paper leaving at least one inch of space between each one. Cut into 1" x 2" strips.

2. Cut the solid blue paper $2\frac{1}{4}$" x $3\frac{3}{4}$", the light blue floral $1\frac{3}{4}$" x $3\frac{1}{4}$", the dark blue floral $1\frac{1}{8}$" x $2\frac{1}{4}$".

3. Layer these pieces as pictured and glue in the center of the notecard.

Guest Book

You'll need:
Purchased journal, 6" x 8"
Ivory paper
Blue solid paper
Light blue floral paper #AG045
  (Anna Griffin)
Dark blue floral paper #AG148
  (Anna Griffin)
14" ivory wire-edge ribbon,
  $1\frac{1}{2}$" wide
Glue gun
Glue stick
Double-sided tape
Font: Edwardian Script

1. Cut the light blue floral paper $6\frac{1}{2}$" x $9\frac{1}{2}$" and four strips $\frac{5}{8}$" x 12".

2. Cut the dark blue floral paper $9\frac{1}{2}$" x $9\frac{1}{2}$".

3. Cut a strip of solid blue paper $2\frac{3}{4}$" x $6\frac{1}{2}$".

4. Print "Guests" on ivory paper or use a stamp or use the words on page 31. Cut it $1\frac{3}{4}$" x $6\frac{1}{2}$" with the word "Guests" 2" from the right edge. Glue the "Guests" strip to the center of the blue strip.

5. Adhere the light blue floral paper to the front of the journal with the glue stick, then wrap the right edge and top and bottom around to the inside and glue, mitering the corners (see page 23).

6. Adhere the dark blue floral paper to the front of the album starting about $3\frac{1}{2}$" from the right hand edge. Wrap around the spine, also adhering with the glue stick and around to the inside back. Miter the corners and adhere to the inside back.

7. Glue the $2\frac{3}{4}$" x $6\frac{1}{2}$" solid blue strip across the front of the album, centered, as pictured. It will come just to the spine.

8. To make the pleats: On the back of the four thin strips of light blue floral paper, mark at top and bottom, every $\frac{1}{4}$" and every 1". Score the paper at these measurements. Fold the first fold forward and the next backwards. Place the four strips together to form one long strip which will be about $13\frac{1}{2}$" long. Adhere a strip of double-sided tape all along the back of this pleated strip joining it together. The double-sided tape will adhere the pleated strip all the way around the album (beginning and ending on the inside).

9. Tie a bow with the wire-edge ribbon and hot glue it to the left edge of the "Guests" strip. Trim the ends and pinch into fan folds.

Program

You'll need:
Ivory paper
Solid blue paper
Blue floral paper #AG148
  (Anna Griffin)
24" light blue sheer ribbon,
  $1\frac{1}{2}$" wide
Font: Edwardian Script

1. Print a title page (add a quote if desired) and 3 other pages – "The Wedding Party", "The Wedding Ceremony", "The Wedding Celebration". Include as much information as you'd like. (See at right for program information and quotes).

2. Cut two pieces of blue floral paper and two solid blue 4" x $5\frac{1}{4}$".

3. Adhere the printed ivory pages to the blue papers.

4. Cut a piece of ribbon $16\frac{1}{4}$". Set the remainder aside.

5. Lay the pages wrong side up on a table starting with the last page and ending with the title page. Leave about $\frac{1}{8}$" between each page.

6. Measure and mark a $2\frac{1}{2}$" area down the middle of the back of the pages. Spread a thin layer of craft glue in this area. Lay the $16\frac{1}{4}$" ribbon into the glue (A). Trim ends if needed.

A

7. Turn right side up (B).

B

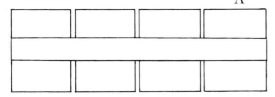

8. Accordion fold the pages with the title page on top (C).

9. Tie the remainder of the ribbon around it and into a bow (D). Trim the ends.

C

D

Suggested Program Quotes

Grow old along with me!
The best is yet to be...
   —Robert Browning

May your hands be forever clasped in friendship and your hearts joined forever in love.
   —Anonymous

I love you not only for what you are, but for what I am when I am with you.
   —Elizabeth Barrett Browning

There is only one happiness in life, to love and be loved.
   —George Sand

God, the best maker of all marriages, Combine your hearts in one.
   —William Shakespeare

In love the paradox occurs that two beings become one and yet remain two.
   —Erich Fromm

And you shall wander hand in hand with love in summer's wonderland.
   —Alfred Noyes

The purpose of a wedding program is to help your guests understand the different aspects of your wedding ceremony so that they feel included.

Wedding programs may include: music, poetry, readings, vows, explanations of special religious rituals, a list of the people who play a significant role in the wedding ceremony, an homage to someone who has passed away, and thanks to those who gave you support.

The program can be as simple or as elaborate as you wish. See the program at left as an example. The program should be passed out by a friend or relative as guests enter the wedding site.

Some alternate ideas:

1. Accordion fold your paper to create the different pages.

2. Form a book with a cover (perhaps with a photograph of you and your fiance.) Add pages by punching holes and threading ribbon through the pages and the cover.

3. Use one simple card with the program information on the front and a bow added to the top.

4. Layer your printed program on a beautiful paper (matching your wedding colors) to form an attractive border.

5. Make a card with a pocket (see invitation on page 17) and include the program information on pages that tuck into the pocket.

Bronze
Brilliance

The honour of your presence is
requested at the marriage of

Meredith Jane Watson

to

Mark David English

Saturday, the Ninth of September

At seven o'clock in the evening

The Double Tree Hotel

456 Highway 101

Del Mar, California

Reception immediately follows

These lovely wedding items capture the color and mood of a radiant autumn day. Shades of burnished bronze are created with the use of brilliant embossing powder. This adds a lustrous shimmer and shine to wedding invitation, favor box, place card and guest book. The votive candle holder is embellished with coordinating bronze ribbon and a dramatic skeleton leaf.

Mike McKinzie

Guests

Bronze Brilliance

Invitation

You'll need:
Brown cardstock
Ivory paper
Scroll border stamp #2481R
  (Anna Griffin)
Light colored ink pad
Embossing powder, Pearlized
  Carnelian (Stampendous)
Embossing heat gun
Craft glue
12" bronze ribbon, $\frac{1}{4}$" wide
Font: Edwardian Script

1. Cut brown cardstock $5\frac{1}{2}$" x 7".

2. Print invitation information on ivory paper and cut to $3\frac{1}{2}$" x $4\frac{3}{4}$".

3. Stamp the design with any light color of ink $\frac{1}{2}$" from the top and bottom of the card and centered side to side. It will help to draw a light pencil line at this mark to line up your stamp. Hint: Complete the inking, stamping and embossing of the top and bottom – one at a time.

4. While the ink is still wet, pour on the embossing powder. Shake off the excess onto a piece of paper and pour back into the container.

5. Heat the stamped areas with the embossing gun. Hold it a little above and keep moving it until you see it start to emboss.

6. Glue the invitation between the two embossed borders.

7. Tie a bow with the ribbon and glue on with craft glue.

Favor Box

You'll need:
Brown cardstock
Scroll border stamp #2481R
  (Anna Griffin)
Embossing powder, Pearlized
  Carnelian (Stampendous)
Heat gun
$\frac{1}{2}$ yd. bronze ribbon, $\frac{1}{4}$" wide
Glue stick

1. Cut the brown cardstock using the template on page 78.

2. Stamp the border design (see photo for position) and follow directions for embossing (steps 3 – 5 of Invitation).

3. Fold into a box and insert tabs into slots. Glue where indicated.

4. Add the favor of your choice and tie with the bronze ribbon.

Make It Easy

Use a pre-made box – open it up and stamp and emboss, then refold and glue back together

More Ideas

Embossing is so much fun, you'll want to create other items using this technique. Try making table numbers, menu cards and your own thank you notes.

For centerpieces, fill terra-cotta pots with an arrangement of bronze-colored mums. Decorate the pots with skeleton leaves and wrap with the same metallic ribbon.

Guest Book

You'll need:
Brown cardstock
Ivory paper
Bronze floral paper
Ivory paper for pages to fill book
Corner stamp #28.025N (Magenta)
Hole punch
Glue stick
Embossing gun
Font: Edwardian Script

1. Cut two pieces of brown cardstock 7" square and several pieces of 7" x 7" ivory paper for the pages.

2. Cut brown floral paper $3\frac{1}{2}$" square and ivory paper $3\frac{3}{4}$" square.

3. Print "Guests" on a piece of ivory paper and cut to 3" square.

4. Follow steps 3 – 5 of Invitation for embossing. Stamp in each corner of one 7" square of brown cardstock. Stamp and apply the embossing powder to each corner separately so that the ink will still be wet when you apply the powder.

5. Glue the $3\frac{3}{4}$" ivory paper in the center of the cover, then center and glue the brown floral paper and the "Guest" paper.

6. Stack the cover, pages and back cover together and punch holes 2" from the top and bottom and about $\frac{1}{4}$" in from the sides.

7. Thread the ribbon through and tie into a bow.

Candle

You'll need:
Frosted glass votive holder
$\frac{1}{2}$" yd. bronze ribbon, $\frac{1}{4}$" wide
3 – 4 bronze skeleton leaves
Craft glue

1. Put a little craft glue on the back of the skeleton leaves. Smooth with your finger and press to the votive holder.
2. Wrap the bronze ribbon around the holder and tie into a bow.

Place Card

You'll need:
Brown cardstock
Ivory paper
Scroll border stamp #2481R
 (Anna Griffin)
Embossing powder, Pearlized
 Carnelian (Stampendous)
Heat gun
Glue stick
Font: Edwardian Script

1. Cut brown card stock $3\frac{1}{2}$" x $5\frac{1}{2}$". Score and fold in half.
2. Print all of the guests' names on ivory paper. Cut them $\frac{5}{8}$" x $3\frac{1}{2}$".
3. Follow the embossing directions (steps 3 through 5 of Invitation). Stamp the design $\frac{1}{4}$" from the fold and from the bottom of the card.
4. Glue the name between the two embossed borders.

Guests

Guests

Guests

Guests

Guests

GUESTS

(May be copied for personal use)

Here's how to emboss a stamped image:

1. Ink the stamp (for best results use a slow drying pigment ink pad).

2. Press the stamp on the paper.

3. Pour the embossing powder on the wet ink. Shake off the excess and save for future projects.

4. Heat over the stamped area using a heat gun until the powder melts and becomes shiny.

5. When using multiple images, do small areas at a time for best results.

Miscellaneous Tips

• When gluing two papers together, glue the pieces together first, than trim them. This will give you neat, even edges.

• Use a bone folder or a credit card to crease your folds. All of your papers will line up better when folds are well creased.

• When tying ribbon around a card, wrap the ribbon around and tie, then turn the card one turn, and tie the bow. The bow will lie correctly and not sideways.

•Self-adhesive monogram stickers can be ordered from a printer. These can be used in many ways—on invitations, envelopes, programs, favor boxes, guest books, match-books, menu cards, place cards, and more.

Guests

Pat Bell

A western collection is ideal for an informal wedding that guarantees a fun time for all. Tied up with rustic twine, the paper items display denim with red and white swirls and dots. Pictured here are the guest book, place card, invitation, save-the-date card and a paper-wrapped favor displaying a covered wagon charm.

SAVE THE DATE

The honour of your presence
is requested at the marriage

Megan Tosca Hill
And
Todd Edward Jones

You are invited to join us as
we exchange our vows
Saturday, the fourteenth of June
At two o'clock in the afternoon

Natural Reflections
110 Live Oak Park Road
San Diego, California

Reception immediately
following the ceremony

Wedding Roundup

Invitation

You'll need:
White cardstock
Blue Chambray paper #61019
  (Memories in the Making)
Red/white dot paper #61014
  (Memories in the Making)
White paper
Coral Spiral vellum #61160
  (Memories in the Making)
10" twine
Glue stick
Glue gun
Font: Times

1. Glue an 8" x 11" piece of denim paper to the same size white cardstock. Score and fold in half.

2. Print invitation information on white paper and cut to 4" x 6".

3. Cut the vellum 4" x 6" and the red dot $4\frac{3}{4}$" x $6\frac{3}{4}$".

4. Glue the invitation to the red dot paper and then both to the denim card.

5. Glue the vellum sheet over the invitation just along the top edge.

6. Tie the twine into a bow and hot glue to the center top of the card.

Save the Date

You'll need:
Blue Chambray paper #61019
  (Memories in the Making)
White cardstock
Ivory mulberry paper
Stamp, "SAVE THE DATE"
  #C2708 (Hero Arts)
Four red eyelets & eyelet setter
24" twine
Red ink pad

1. Glue a 5" x 7" denim piece to the same size cardstock piece. Score and fold in half. Print the wedding information.

2. Position the eyelets in each corner of the card and attach using the eyelet setter.

3. Stamp a piece of the mulberry paper with "Save the Date" with red ink. Tear around all edges so that the paper measures approximately 1" x 3". Glue this piece in the center of the card on an angle.

4. Thread the twine through the eyelets and tie in a bow at the top.

Favor

You'll need:
Red/white check napkin
Candy of choice
Twine
Covered wagon charm
  (Creative Beginnings)
Glue gun

1. Lay the napkin on a flat surface with wrong side facing up. Place candy of choice (Red Hots, Hot Tamales, or red and white jelly beans, for instance) in the center.

2. Gather up the napkin around the candy and wrap with twine. Slip the charm onto the twine and tie into a bow.

Guest Book

You'll need:
Purchased journal 5" x 8"
Blue Chambray #61019
  (Memories in the Making)
Red/white Dot paper #61014
  (Memories in the Making)
Red/white Spiral paper #61154
  (Memories in the Making)
Ivory paper
Red/white check napkin
Two red eyelets and eyelet setter
12" twine
Glue stick
Font: Times

1. Cut the denim paper 6" x 10". Glue to the front cover of the journal. Wrap the right edges and top and bottom edges to the inside of the cover and glue.

2. Cut the red spiral paper $1\frac{1}{2}$" x 3" and the red dot paper using the pattern on page 78 for the pocket.

3. Print "Guests" on the ivory paper and tear around the edges to approximately 1" x $3\frac{1}{2}$".

4. Cut the denim into a triangle $1\frac{1}{2}$" x 3" for flap (pattern on page 78).

5. Fold the top edge of the flap under $\frac{1}{4}$". Position the flap onto the red dot pocket and glue. Fasten a red eyelet in each corner of the flap using the eyelet setter.

6. Glue the pocket to the front of the book leaving the top open (refer to photo for placement).

7. Cut one corner of the napkin into a triangle and glue to the opening of the pocket.

8. Glue the "Guests" piece to the red spiral piece and then glue to the top of the book.

9. Tie the twine into a bow and hot glue to the spiral piece.

Place Card

You'll need:
Blue Chambray paper #61019
  (Memories in the Making)
White cardstock
Red/white Spiral paper
  (Memories in the Making)
White mulberry paper
Calligraphy pen
6" twine
Glue gun and glue sticks

1. Glue a $3\frac{1}{4}$" x 4" denim piece to the same size cardstock piece. Score and fold in half.

2. Cut the red/spiral paper $2\frac{3}{4}$" x $1\frac{1}{2}$" and glue to the center of the denim card.

3. Tear around the edges of the mulberry paper to measure approximately 1" x 2". Center this piece on the card and glue in place.

4. Write guest's name on the mulberry paper using a calligraphy pen.

5. Tie a small bow of twine and hot glue to the upper left corner of the card.

Save the Date

Save the Date

Save the Date

Save the Date

Save the Date

(May be copied for personal use.)

More Ideas

Use red check tablecloths for the reception tables.
• Add small bales of hay as centerpieces.
• Create table number cards by gluing twine in the shape of numbers on blue denim cardstock. Attach the cards to a wire poke and insert in the hay.
• Use red bandannas as napkins instead of the paper napkins.

It's important to decide on a wedding theme early in your planning. This will help in your choice of dress, flowers, colors, wedding site, invitations, etc.

Some of the ideas in this book lend themselves to theme weddings such as the western ideas on the preceding page or the seaside projects on page 12.

Some other theme weddings might include:

Candlelight

Winter

Autumn

Spring

Christmas

New Years

Valentine's Day

Irish

Asian

Latin-American

African-American

Renaissance

Victorian

English Garden

Princess or fairy tale

Nautical

Butterfly

Jungle

Roaring 20s

Rock 'n Roll

Movie theme - the wedding is based on a favorite romantic movie such as Casa Blanca or An Affair to Remember.

Think how much fun it will be to design all of your wedding elements around a theme. It will make your planning so much easier.

Romantic Roses

The rose is considered the "Queen of the flowers" and symbolizes romance. What better flower to adorn every element of a wedding—from the shower invitation to the wedding invitation, the guest book, place card, favor and the paper-wrapped candle holder.

Mike McKinzie

The honour of your presence
Is requested at the marriage of
Patricia Ann Cummins
And
Matthew Alan Scott
Saturday, the Sixteenth of June
At six o'clock in the evening
Wilshire Presbyterian Church
3600 Wilshire Boulevard
Los Angeles, California
Reception immediately follows

Romantic Roses

Invitation

You'll need:
Burgundy cardstock
Gold paper (Shizen)
Ivory paper
Deckle edge scissors
Rose sticker #64188 Victorian
   Memories (Memories in Making)
6" burgundy wire-edged ombre
   ribbon, 1" wide
Glue stick
Craft glue
Font: Edwardian Script

1. Cut burgundy cardstock 7" x 10". Score and fold in half.

2. Tear the gold paper to approximately $4\frac{1}{2}$" x $6\frac{1}{2}$".

3. Cut the ivory paper $2\frac{3}{4}$" x $5\frac{1}{4}$" and adhere to the gold paper about $\frac{1}{2}$" from the right edge.

4. Print the invitation information on vellum making sure that it will fit in approximately $2\frac{1}{2}$" x $4\frac{3}{4}$". Cut this vellum with a deckle edge scissors to 3" x $5\frac{1}{2}$". Glue this to the top edge of the ivory paper.

5. Attach the rose sticker as pictured.

6. Tie the ribbon in a knot and notch the ends. Glue to the left hand side of the gold paper.

Shower Invitation

You'll need:
Burgundy cardstock
Gold paper (Shizen)
Ivory paper
Words Sepia paper #61225
   (Memories in the Making)
Large Rose sticker #66057 Rose
   Frames (Memories in the Making)
Glue stick
Font: Edwardian Script

1. Cut the burgundy cardstock 7" x 10", score and fold in half.

2. Cut the "words" paper $4\frac{1}{4}$" x $5\frac{1}{4}$" and adhere to the cardstock $\frac{3}{8}$" from the top and sides leaving $1\frac{1}{2}$" at the bottom.

3. Attach the rose sticker centered and toward the top of this paper (Use just the center section of the rose sticker.)

4. Tear the gold paper to about $1\frac{1}{2}$" x $3\frac{3}{4}$" and glue to the bottom of the "words" paper (see photo).

5. Print "You're Invited" on ivory paper. Cut to $\frac{1}{2}$" x 2" and glue in the middle of the gold paper.

Guest Book

You'll need:
Purchased album, burgundy velvet
   cover (6" x 9")
Gold paper (Shizen)
Ivory paper
Rose sticker #64188 Victorian
   Memories (Memories in Making)
Glue stick
Deckle edge scissors
Font: Edwardian Script

1. Tear the gold paper to approximately $2\frac{1}{2}$" x 4" and adhere to the album front, centered and about 1" from the right edge.

2. Print "Guests" on ivory paper or copy the words from page 31 and cut with deckle edge scissors to $1\frac{1}{2}$" x $2\frac{1}{2}$". Glue to the gold paper (as pictured) leaving room for the rose sticker.

3. Apply the rose sticker on the left side.

Place Card

You'll need:
Burgundy cardstock
Gold paper (Shizen)
Ivory paper
Rose sticker #64188 Victorian
   Memories (Memories in Making)
Glue stick
Deckle edge scissors
Font: Edwardian Script

1. Cut the burgundy cardstock 4" x 4". Score and fold in half.

2. Tear the gold paper to approximatey $1\frac{1}{2}$" x $3\frac{1}{2}$" and adhere to the cardstock.

3. Print all the guests' names on ivory paper, leaving enough room between them for cutting. Cut with a deckle edge scissors 1" x $2\frac{1}{2}$". Adhere to the gold paper.

4. Apply the rose sticker in the upper left hand corner.

Candle

You'll need:
Square glass votive candle holder
Burgundy mulberry paper (Shizen)
Gold paper (Shizen)
Square hole punch
Glue stick

1. Cut strips of burgundy paper $1\frac{1}{4}$" x $2\frac{1}{2}$".

2. Cut strips of gold paper 1" x $9\frac{1}{2}$". Cut one edge with a straight edge and tear the other edge.

3. Punch holes all around with the square hole punch. Punch on an angle to create diamond-shaped holes. Adhere this to the burgundy strip.

4. Wrap it around the votive holder, overlap and adhere with the glue stick.

Favor

You'll need:
Burgundy mulberry paper
White paper lace doily, 6"
Gold tissue
Rose sticker #64188 Victorian
  Memories (Memories in Making)
Glue stick

1. Cut the burgundy paper 4" square.

2. Fold up each edge 1". Unfold, and at each corner there will be a folded area 1" square. Put glue in this area (A). Pinch each glued corner together (B). Add glue to each of these triangular flaps and fold them into the opposing sides of the box (C).

3. Apply a rose sticker on one side of the box.

4. Fold the doily in the same way as you did the burgundy paper (D). Open it up. Pinch the corners and push to the inside (E). This time you won't need glue. Push this into the burgundy box.

5. Place a bon-bon or truffle in the middle of the gold tissue square and insert into the doily.

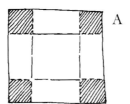

A

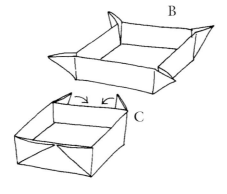

B

C

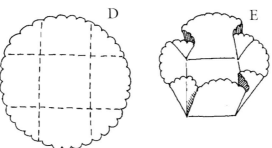

D   E

Tearing the edges of paper adds texture and dimension to cards which gives the final project a very unique look. Here's how:

1. Determine the direction of the grain by taking a small scrap and tearing it in each direction. Tearing with the grain will seem easier. Then decide which look you like best, with or against the grain. Each will have a slightly different look.

2. If using handmade paper, it helps to moisten it first. This makes the fibers easier to separate and will give the paper a soft interesting edge. Hold the paper with one hand and tear toward you with the other.

3. Optional: draw a light pencil line on the paper before tearing to give a more defined look.

4. Different types of paper will give different effects when torn. Experiment to get the best results.

5. Mulberry paper reveals interesting fibers when torn. To tear mulberry paper, fold along the edge to be torn. Use a small wet paintbrush and moisten along the fold. Separate the paper along the fold. This will separate the fibers for a soft, textured look.

Most tearing is done by hand. But there are rulers available for tearing that have different types of edges. To use a ruler, press the ruler down on the paper and tear toward you.

This beautiful assortment of wedding projects must have been touched by Midas. The unique paper used for the invitation is embedded with tiny golden threads. The other projects include gold seals stamped with the couple's initial. Seen here are the invitation, a favor, a gift box for the bridal attendants and a reply card.

Golden Ceremony

N

We look forward to
Celebrating with you
Please reply by October 18, 2004
Name _____

_____ will attend
_____ not able to attend

Invitation

You'll need:
White/gold paper (Shizen)
Gold paper (Shizen)
Ivory paper
Gold wax
Seal with initial
Glue stick
Font: Edwardian Script

1. Score the $8\frac{1}{2}$"x 11" white/gold paper at each short edge $2\frac{1}{2}$" in. Fold these "doors" in and press firmly.

2. Cut the gold paper $5\frac{1}{2}$" x $8\frac{1}{2}$". Apply glue along the top edge. Open the white/gold paper and adhere the gold paper to the middle section.

3. Print the invitation information on the ivory paper and cut it to $3\frac{1}{2}$" x $6\frac{1}{2}$". Apply glue along the top edge and adhere it to the center of the gold paper.

4. Cut a 2" square of gold paper and a $1\frac{1}{2}$" square of white/gold paper. Center and glue the white paper to the gold paper.

5. Turn this layered piece on a diagonal so that it becomes a diamond shape. Apply the sealing wax to the center of the white square. Press the initial stamp into the hot wax. (Practice this first on a piece of scrap paper.)

6. After the wax has hardened, turn the square over and apply glue to the right hand half of the diamond shape. Adhere it to the center edge of the left hand "door" (see photo).

Gift for Attendants

You'll need:
Purchased white corrugated pillow box 7" x 12"
Gold paper (Shizen)
White/gold paper (Shizen)
20" gold sheer ribbon, $1\frac{1}{2}$" wide
Gold wax
Seal with initial
Glue stick
Transparent tape

1. Cut gold paper 3" square and white/gold paper $1\frac{1}{2}$" square. Center and adhere the white paper to the gold.

2. Turn the paper diagonally so that it becomes a diamond shape. Apply the sealing wax to the center and press the initial stamp into the hot wax.

3. Place the gift in the box.

4. Wrap the gold ribbon around the box and secure in back with tape.

5. Apply glue to the whole back of the layered paper and press onto the front of the box over the ribbon.

Favor Box

You'll need:
Purchased white box with handles 3" x $4\frac{1}{2}$"
Gold paper (Shizen)
White/gold paper (Shizen)
Gold wax
Seal with initial
$\frac{1}{2}$ yd. gold ribbon, $\frac{1}{4}$" wide
White petals

1. Follow the previous directions for making the layered paper and sealing wax, but cut the gold paper $1\frac{3}{4}$" square and the white paper $1\frac{1}{4}$" square.

2. Punch a hole at the top of the diamond shape. Wrap gold ribbon around the bag and through the hole. Tie into a bow. Secure the ribbon at the back of the bag with tape.

3. Fill the box with rose petals. These should be placed on a table as the guests go into the ceremony. The rose petals are scattered as the couple leave.

Reply Card

You'll need:
White/gold paper (Shizen)
Gold paper (Shizen)
Ivory paper
Gold initial sticker #64026 (Memories in the Making)
Glue stick
Font: Edwardian Script

1. Print the information on the white paper and cut to $2\frac{1}{2}$" x $4\frac{1}{4}$".

2. Cut the white/gold paper $3\frac{1}{8}$" x $4\frac{3}{4}$", the gold paper $2\frac{3}{4}$" x $4\frac{1}{4}$". Adhere together with the glue stick.

3. Adhere the ivory printed piece to the gold paper.

Optional: Add an initial sticker in the upper left hand corner.

(See page 51 for instructions and tips for using sealing wax and seals.)

A tray filled with an assortment of glowing tea lights decorates an Asian themed wedding. See the following pages for an east/west inspired invitation, menu card, shower invitation, place card, favor and attendant's gift.

The honour of your presence
Is requested at the marriage of

Anne Mae Rafferty
And
Lee Hondo

Saturday, the Sixteenth of June
At six o'clock in the evening

New Otoni Hotel
560 First Avenue
Los Angeles, California

Reception immediately follows

Anne & Lee

East meets West

Drama is added to this wedding assortment with exotic Asian-inspired papers. This handsome set includes the clever take-out carton for the attendant's gift, the decorated bag filled with fortune cookies for a favor, place card, shower invitation, wedding invitation and menu card.

Betty Taft

Anne & Lee
Menu
Appetizers
Hamachi Sashimi on Wanton Chard
With Ogo Seaweed Salad and Red Topiko Caviar
Thai Chicken Wonton Purse
Served with Spicy Peanut Sauce

Soup
Artichoke Soup

Salad
Watermelon, Tomato and Cucumber Salad
With Sweet Sesame Vinaigrette

Entrée
Orange Glazed Barbecued Halibut
With Summer Herb-Blackberry Reduction
Grilled Asparagus and Yukon Gold Potato Risotto

Dessert
Caramelized Pear Tart with Almond Cream

Shower Invitation

You'll need:
Natural ivory cardstock (Shizen)
Asian calligraphy paper
  (Loose Ends)
Lavender tissue paper
Dark green silk paper (Shizen)
Japanese origami paper
Japanese paper cord, various colors
  (Mizuhiki by Yasutomo)
Craft knife
Small hole punch
Glue stick

1. Cut the ivory cardstock 6" x 9". Score and fold in half.

2. Cut the calligraphy paper $3\frac{1}{2}$" x 4", the lavender paper $2\frac{1}{2}$" x 3", the green $1\frac{3}{4}$" x 2" and the origami paper $\frac{3}{4}$" x $3\frac{1}{2}$".

3. Cut two slits with a craft knife in the green paper $\frac{3}{4}$" wide and $\frac{1}{2}$" from the top and bottom of the paper. Slide the origami paper strip through the slits.

4. Layer the papers as shown in the photo and apply with the glue stick.

5. Open the card and punch a small hole in the middle on the fold. Thread three pieces of 15" long cord through the hole to wrap around the front of the card. Tie in a square knot.

6. Handwrite the invitation details on the inside or print on paper using your computer and printer and glue to the inside.

Wedding Invitation

You'll need:
Natural ivory cardstock (Shizen)
Lavender silk paper
Ivory paper
Japanese origami paper
Glue stick
Font: Papyrus

1. Cut the natural paper 5" x $7\frac{1}{2}$", the lavender silk $3\frac{3}{4}$" x 6" and the origami paper into two strips $\frac{1}{2}$" x $1\frac{1}{2}$" and $\frac{1}{2}$" x $1\frac{3}{4}$".

2. Print the invitation information on ivory paper and cut to $3\frac{3}{8}$" x $5\frac{1}{2}$".

3. Glue the lavender paper and the invitation to the natural paper using the glue stick with just a strip of glue across the top.

4. Glue the two origami strips as shown in the photo.

Place Card

You'll need
Natural ivory cardstock (Shizen)
Ivory paper
Lavender silk paper (Shizen)
Japanese origami paper
Calligraphy pen
Glue stick

1. Cut the ivory paper $3\frac{1}{2}$" x 4". Score and fold in half.

2. Cut the lavender paper $1\frac{1}{4}$" x $2\frac{3}{4}$", center and glue to the ivory paper.

3. Cut another piece of ivory paper $\frac{1}{2}$" x 2" and glue to the lower portion of the lavender paper. Write the name using a calligraphy pen.

4. Cut the origami paper into a 1" square.

5. Glue the square on the diagonal so that half of it extends above the fold.

Menu Card

You'll need:
Natural ivory cardstock (Shizen)
Lavender mulberry paper
Ivory paper
Japanese origami paper
Font: Papyrus

1. Cut the handmade natural paper $7\frac{1}{2}$" x 10", the lavender paper 6" x $8\frac{1}{2}$" and the origami paper into a $1\frac{1}{2}$" square.

2. Print the menu on the ivory paper and cut 5" x $7\frac{1}{2}$".

3. Layer the lavender paper and menu on the natural paper and adhere with a glue stick just at the top.

4. Cut the origami paper in half diagonally, forming two triangles. Glue these at the top and bottom of the menu card as shown in the photograph.

5. Display menu cards in the center of each table on small easels.

Tea Lights

You'll need:
Ivory tea lights
Paper
Japanese calligraphy paper
  (Loose Ends)
Japanese origami paper
Glue stick

1. Cut the calligraphy paper into $\frac{3}{4}$" x 5" strips (or to fit around the tea lights you'll be using).
2. Cut the origami paper into $\frac{3}{4}$" squares.
3. Glue the calligraphy paper around each tea light using a glue stick. Glue the square of origami paper over the seam of the calligraphy paper.

(Use the tea lights in groups placed on a tray or place one by each table setting.)

Attendant's Gift Box

You'll need:
Vellum take-out carton
Japanese origami paper
Lavender paper
Ivory paper
Glue stick
Font: Papyrus

1. Cut the lavender paper 2" square and the origami paper $1\frac{1}{4}$" square.
2. Print the bride and groom's name on ivory paper and cut into $\frac{1}{2}$" wide strips and as long as needed to fit the names.
3. Glue the squares together with the name tag glued across the diagonal.
4. Glue this layered paper to the carton on a diagonal.
5. Place the gift in the carton.

Favor Bag

You'll need:
Purchased bright colored "lunch bags" about 3" x 6"
  (Mrs. Grossman's)
Lavender paper
Green silk paper (Shizen)
Japanese origami paper
Japanese paper cord
  (Mizuhiki by Yasutomo)
Small round hole punch
Glue stick

1. Cut the green paper $1\frac{1}{4}$" square, the lavender $1\frac{3}{4}$" square and the origami $\frac{7}{8}$" square.
2. Layer and glue the three squares as pictured.
3. Fill the bag with fortune cookies or a favor of your choice.
4. Fold the top of the bag down about 2". Glue the layered papers to the top of the fold.
5. Punch two small holes through the papers at the center and thread the cord through. Tie in a square knot.

• If you're having out of town guests, make up a pretty gift box for their hotel/motel room. Include snacks, fresh fruit, bottled water, a map of your town (see your Chamber of Commerce for pamphlets about other points of interest in your area), TV Guide and a schedule of the wedding events planned. Decorate the box with pretty papers that coordinate with your theme. The label might read:

Welcome to Mike and Jane's
wedding events

or

Thank you for sharing this
special time with us

Mike and Jane

• For the reception restrooms, decorate a box (again to coordinate with the theme of your wedding). For the ladies room include: perfume or cologne, a sewing kit, safety pins, clear nail polish (in case of nylon runs) hand lotion, breath spray and mints. For the men's room, spray cologne for men, breath spray and mints, lint brush and shoe buffing cloth.

• After your wedding, have twelve of your favorite photographs made into a calendar (at your local print shop) and give copies to your family members as Christmas gifts.

Thank You

Thank you for sharing our joy

The gleaming and luminous surface of these gold embossed accessories will surely attract attention. The wedding invitation, thank you note, place card and CD cover radiate opulence and visual appeal. The bubbles are wrapped in sheer ivory tulle and finished with a glimmering golden ribbon.

Edged in Gold

Invitation

You'll need:
Ivory/gold embossed (Shizen)
Ivory paper
White vellum
Gold ink pad
12" white sheer ribbon with gold trim, $\frac{1}{2}$" wide
Glue stick
Glue gun
Font: Edwardian Script

1. Cut gold/ivory embossed paper 8" x 11". Score and fold in half.

2. Print the wedding information on ivory paper. Cut to 4" x 6".

3. Cut the vellum paper 4" x 6". Place the vellum on the printed ivory paper. Use a penny as a template to mark and cut each corner of both papers.

4. Rub the edges of the vellum using the gold ink pad.

5. Center and adhere the printed ivory paper to the front of the card.

6. Layer the vellum on the ivory paper and glue along the top edge using a glue stick.

7. Tie the ribbon into a bow and adhere to the invitation using a glue gun.

Place Card

You'll need:
Purchased place cards, 2" x 3"
Gold ink pad
6" white sheer ribbon with gold trim, $\frac{1}{2}$" wide
Gold calligraphy pen (optional)
Glue gun

1. Rub the edges of the place card with the gold ink pad.

2. Write the guest's name on the card.

3. Tie the ribbon into a bow and adhere to the card using a glue gun.

Thank You Note

You'll need:
Purchased embossed ivory card 3$\frac{1}{2}$" x 5"
White vellum
Gold ink pad
Glue stick
Font: Edwardian Script

1. Use your finger tip to rub the gold ink on the card's embossed edge.

2. Print "Thank you" on the vellum paper several times (leave enough space to cut out a 1$\frac{1}{2}$" x 3$\frac{1}{2}$" piece).

3. Use a penny for a template to mark, then cut each corner of the card.

4. Rub the edge of the vellum with the gold ink pad.

5. Affix this piece to the center of the card using a glue stick.

CD Holder

You'll need:
Gold/ivory embossed (Shizen)
White vellum
Gold ink pad
Velcro® dots
Glue stick
Font: Edwardian Script

1. Cut gold and ivory paper 7" x 11".

2. Score and fold the long edges under 1".

3. Score and fold the bottom edge of the paper up 3$\frac{1}{2}$". Glue each side to hold.

4. Score and fold the top edge of the paper down 2$\frac{1}{2}$".

5. Adhere the Velcro® dots under the flap to keep closed.

6. Print the message on vellum paper several times. Cut out each piece to measure 1$\frac{1}{2}$" x 2". Use a dime as a template to mark and cut each corner.

7. Rub the edges of the vellum using the gold ink pad.

8. Adhere the vellum just to the top of the flap using a glue stick.

Bubbles

You'll need:
Bottle of bubbles
White tulle
6" gold ribbon, 1" wide

1. Cut the tulle into an 8" square. Place the bottle in the center and gather up the sides.

2. Wrap the ribbon around and tie into a bow. Trim the tulle if necessary.

Making a musical CD for a wedding favor.

A really special favor for your guests is a musical CD full of songs that are meaningful to you and your fiancee. Here's how to do it:

1. Sit down as a couple and make a list of your favorites. It's best to record about 12 songs.

2. When your list is finalized, purchase blank CDs from a computer store. We've given you instructions for making your own covers (see pages 50 and 77), but if you don't have time, you can purchase jewel cases to hold the CDs. You might decide to design your own insert for the case.

3. You need a CD burner on your computer to make CDs. You can download the songs or copy them from your own CDs or LPs. Follow the manual to your CD burner to continue.

4. Listen to the completed CD to make sure everything has copied correctly. Make any corrections before you make your multiple copies.

You can purchase blank CD labels at paper stores. Or you can also have them made professionally by the following company:

www.weddingcd.cdbyme.com

They will create custom-made labels for you. They have a huge variety of designs available, and will also include your photograph on the labels.

Be sure to observe copyright laws when recording your CDs.

Thank you for sharing our joy

Thank you for sharing our wedding day

A selection of our favorite music

A selection of our favorite music

(May be copied for personal use.)

A personal seal will lend dignity, prestige and a personal flair to your wedding invitations and accessories.

1. Use a cotton swab to apply a small amount of oil to your seal so that no wax will adhere to it.

2. Holding the stick at a 45° angle, light the wick, just as you would a candle. Drip enough wax on the seal area. The amount of wax depends on the size of the seal. By changing the angle of the stick slightly you can adjust the flow of the melting wax.

3. Blow out the flame when there is enough wax on the paper. Take the underside of the stick and blend the melted wax in a circular fashion to create a lovely smooth edge.

4. With metallic colors, wait several seconds before applying the seal. On non-metallic colors, you can press the seal immediately. Hold it firmly, but briefly, then pull the seal up.

Have the post office hand-cancel your envelopes to avoid the automated sorting machines.

You can have a custom monogram seal made. For information see:

www.nostalgicimpressions.com

You can make 10 – 12 impressions from a normal 4" sealing wax stick.

Tip: To avoid any unnecessary spills or messes on your finished invitations, make your seals on wax paper. Transfer the cooled seal to your invitation or envelope and glue it on.

Sealing wax is not recommended for use by young children.

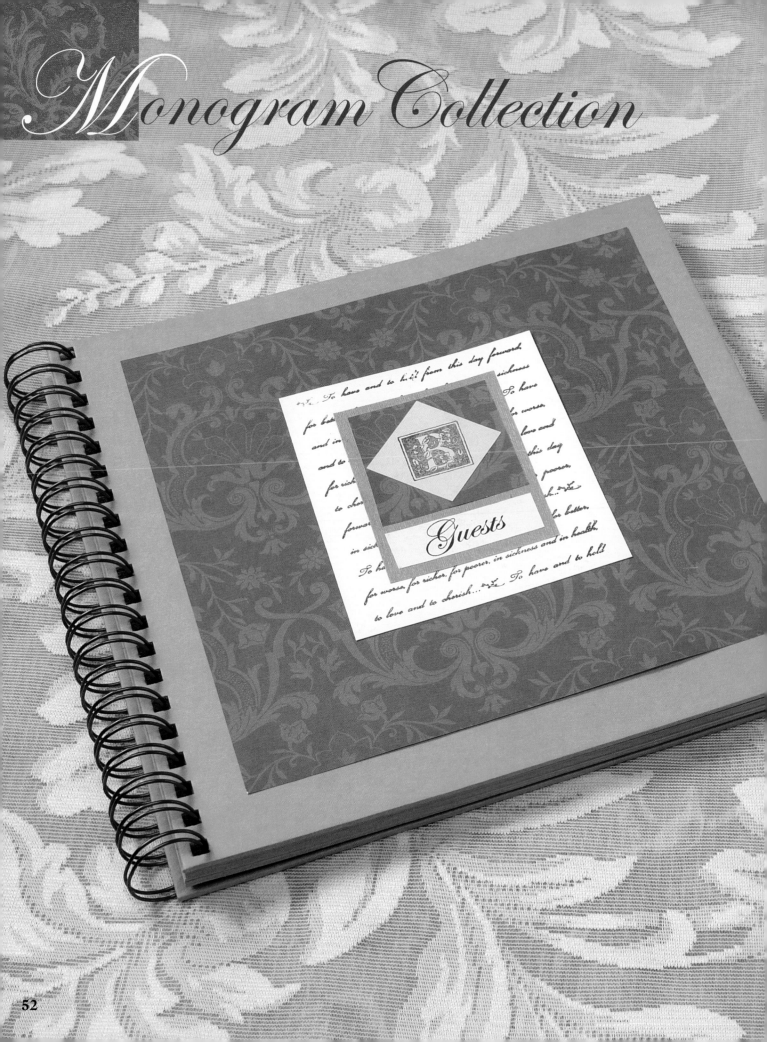

Guests

These handsome wedding items are all adorned with a beautiful stamped monogram. What better way to announce the upcoming event. The background of the invitation and guest book are stamped with lovely romantic calligraphy. Rubber stamping is an ideal technique for creating multiple paper items. Pictured here are the guest book, invitation, reply card, attendant gift bag and little favor box including a delicious chocolate truffle.

We look forward to
Celebrating with you
Please reply by: October 18, 2004
Name _____

_____ will attend
_____ not able to attend

Monogram Collection

Invitation

You'll need:
Ivory cardstock
Ivory paper
Gold paper (Shizen)
Burgundy floral paper #AG002
   (Anna Griffin)
Pink solid paper
Wedding Word Print stamp #S1390
   (Hero Arts)
Alphabet "B" stamp #B2014
   (Stamparosa)
Brown ink pad
12" gold sheer ribbon, $1\frac{1}{2}$" wide
Glue stick

1. Cut the ivory cardstock $5\frac{1}{2}$" x 8", score and fold in half.

2. Stamp the "Wedding Word Print" design using brown ink on the front of card. (Hint: practice stamping first on a piece of scrap paper. On a large stamp such as this, press firmly all over the whole stamp.)

3. Cut the following squares: $2\frac{1}{2}$" of the gold, $2\frac{1}{4}$" of the burgundy and $1\frac{1}{2}$" of the pink. Turn the pink square diagonally so that it becomes a diamond.

4. Stamp the initial with brown ink in the center of the pink diamond shape.

5. Glue the pink diamond to the burgundy square and then to the gold square.

6. Cut the gold ribbon 11" long and wrap it around from the inside to the front of the card. Join the ends neatly in the center front of the card. Don't overlap. Secure with a glue stick.

7. Glue the layered monogram label over the place where the ribbon ends join.

8. Print the invitation information on ivory paper and cut 4" x $5\frac{1}{2}$". Glue to the inside of the card.

Guest Book

You'll need:
Purchased scrapbook, 10" x 10"
Burgundy floral paper #AG002
   (Anna Griffin)
Ivory paper
Gold paper (Shizen)
Pink solid paper
Wedding Word Print stamp #S1390
   (Hero Arts)
Alphabet "B" stamp #B2014
   (Stamparosa)
Brown ink pad
Glue stick
Font: Edwardian Script

1. Cut burgundy paper $8\frac{1}{2}$" square and another square $2\frac{1}{4}$". Cut the ivory paper $4\frac{1}{4}$" x 5". Cut pink paper $1\frac{1}{2}$" square and gold paper $2\frac{1}{2}$" x $3\frac{1}{2}$".

2. Stamp the "Wedding Word Print" on the ivory paper (practice first following instructions for stamping on page 15). Set aside to dry.

3. Turn the pink square on the diagonal to form a diamond and stamp the initial in the center using brown ink.

4. Glue the large square of burgundy paper centered on the front of the journal. Then center the stamped ivory paper and glue on top. Next center and glue the gold paper. Glue the small burgundy square at the top of the gold paper leaving an equal border at top and sides and a larger area at the bottom (see photo). Next, glue on the pink diamond shape with the initial centered in the burgundy square.

5. Print "Guests" on a sheet of ivory paper and cut $\frac{3}{4}$" x $2\frac{1}{4}$" (or copy it from page 31). Glue at bottom of gold paper with an equal border all around.

Reply Card

You'll need:
Gold paper
Burgundy floral paper #AG002
   (Anna Griffin)
Ivory paper
Glue stick
Font: Edwardian Script

1. Cut the gold paper $2\frac{3}{4}$" x $4\frac{1}{2}$", the burgundy paper $2\frac{1}{4}$" x 4".

2. Print the information on the ivory paper and cut to $2\frac{1}{8}$" x $3\frac{3}{4}$".

3. Layer the three papers and glue together.

About Reply Cards

The reply card or RSVP, (French for "Repondez s'il vous plait") lets you know how many will be coming to your wedding and reception. Insert the card inside the flap of a self addressed, stamped envelope. Then it should be placed with the envelope face down on top of your invitation along with any other enclosures such as direction cards, accommodation cards, etc.

If you aren't having the reply envelopes printed, check with a local rubber stamp store. They can have a special stamp made with your name and address—just perfect for making your self-addressed envelopes. Choose a font that closely matches the one on your invitation.

Gift Bag

You'll need:
Gold paper
Burgundy floral paper #AG002
 (Anna Griffin)
Pink solid paper
Alphabet "B" stamp #B2014
 (Stamparosa)
Brown ink pad
16" gold ribbon, $\frac{1}{4}$" wide
Glue stick

1. To make the bag: Cut the gold paper $4\frac{3}{4}$" x $9\frac{1}{2}$".
2. Score it $1\frac{1}{2}$" from each short end and again $1\frac{1}{2}$" from that (A).

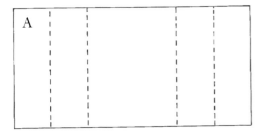

3. Fold on the score lines and glue together overlapping $\frac{1}{4}$" at the back (B).

4. At one end, push in on each side as if you were wrapping a gift (C). Fold in and glue to two points that will be created when you do this (D). This will form the bottom of the bag.

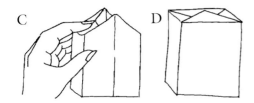

5. Embellishing the bag: Cut burgundy paper $1\frac{3}{4}$" square, cut pink paper $1\frac{1}{4}$" square.
6. Stamp the initial on the pink square using brown ink.

7. Turn the burgundy square on the diagonal so that it forms a diamond and glue the pink square in the center.
8. Place a piece of jewelry or other small gift in the bag. Turn down the top (E) and wrap the gold ribbon around it and tie into a bow at the top. Glue the initial label over the ribbon.

Favor Box

You'll need:
Burgundy floral paper #AG002
(Anna Griffin)
Pink paper
Gold tissue paper
Decorative corner punch
 (Anna Griffin)
Glue stick
Scallop edge scissors

1. Cut four pink squares $1\frac{1}{2}$" each.
2. Cut the burgundy floral paper $4\frac{1}{2}$" square. Punch each corner with the decorative punch.
3. Measure and score $1\frac{1}{2}$" in on all sides (A).
4. Cut in $1\frac{1}{2}$" on every other score (B).

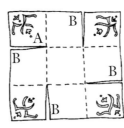

5. Glue the four pink squares as indicated (C).
6. Place glue on the front of each pink square and fold up into a box so that the punched squares overlap the pink squares. Press each glued area to secure (D & E).

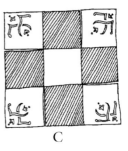

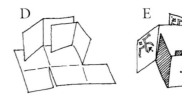

7. Cut a $4\frac{1}{2}$" square of gold tissue paper with a scallop edge scissors. Place a truffle in the tissue and place in the box with the tissue extending above.

Make it Easy

Look for pre-cut colored squares from Color Bok. These little gems are a real time saver. Just stamp or punch and glue to your projects.

Harlequin

Mary Smith

A harlequin design forms the base of these chic cards of black and gold. A touch of unexpected lavender appears on the shower invitation. Black and gold leafy handmade paper decorates the favor box and the tissue-wrapped bubbles.

Harlequin

Invitation

You'll need:

Ivory cardstock
Gold corrugated paper (Shizen)
Black/gold print paper (Shizen)
Taupe cardstock
Harlequin stamp #3218F
  (Rubber Stampede)
Bride and groom stamp #J118
  (Stampendous)
Gold ink pad
Black ink pad
Glue stick

1. Cut the ivory cardstock $5\frac{1}{2}$" x $8\frac{1}{2}$". Score and fold in half.

2. Cut the black paper $1\frac{1}{2}$" x $2\frac{1}{8}$", the gold corrugated $1\frac{1}{4}$" x $1\frac{3}{4}$" and the taupe paper 1" x $1\frac{3}{8}$".

3. In the center of the card, measure and mark lightly with a pencil an area the size of the Harlequin stamp (2" x 3").

4. Ink the stamp with gold ink and stamp.

5. Stamp the "bride and groom" design with black ink on the taupe cardstock.

6. Layer and glue the papers as shown in the photograph.

7. Print invitation information on ivory paper and glue to inside.

Shower Invitation

You'll need:

Ivory cardstock
Purple mulberry
Lavender floral paper #AG231
  (Anna Griffin)
Harlequin stamp #3218
  (Rubber Stampede)
12" black and white check
  ribbon $\frac{1}{2}$" wide
6" purple sheer ribbon, $1\frac{1}{2}$" wide
Glue stick

1. Cut the ivory cardstock $5\frac{1}{2}$" x 8". Score and fold. Cut the purple mulberry paper $2\frac{1}{2}$" x $5\frac{1}{2}$". Tear one long edge.

2. Stamp the Harlequin design using black ink on another piece of ivory cardstock and cut closely around the edge.

3. Cut the heart out of the lavender floral paper using the pattern on page 59.

4. Glue the purple mulberry paper to the left hand side of the card.

5. Cut the gold ribbon 12" long. Glue this around the front of the card and onto inside. Overlap the ends or cut them so they exactly meet.

6. Glue the Harlequin paper over the ribbon and then the heart on top (refer to photograph).

7. Write the shower information on the inside of the card.

8. Tie the check ribbon around the whole card and tie in a knot over the heart.

Favor

You'll need:

3" round papier mache box
Gold corrugated paper
Black/gold paper (Shizen)
Gold acrylic paint
Paintbrush
16" gold ribbon, $\frac{1}{4}$" wide
Craft glue
Glue stick

1. Paint the bottom section of the box gold.

2. Use the top of the box as a template to trace around onto the back of the black/gold paper. Cut out this circle.

3. Glue the black paper to the top of the box.

4. Cut a strip of the gold corrugated $\frac{1}{2}$" x 11". Glue this around the rim of the box using craft glue. Trim where the two ends meet.

5. Add the favor and then wrap the gold ribbon around the box and into a bow on the top.

Place Card

You'll need:

Purchased white place card, 2" x $3\frac{1}{4}$"
Ivory paper
Black/gold paper (Shizen)
Harlequin stamp #3218F
  (Rubber Stampede)
Gold ink pad
Calligraphy pen
Glue stick

1. Stamp the Harlequin stamp with gold ink on a piece of ivory paper. Cut it $1\frac{1}{2}$" x $2\frac{3}{4}$".

2. Cut the black paper 1" x 2" and another piece of ivory paper $\frac{3}{4}$" x $1\frac{3}{4}$".

3. Center and glue the black paper on the card and the ivory paper over it.

4. Use a fine pointed calligraphy pen to write the guests' names.

Bubbles

You'll need:

White/gold harlequin tissue paper
Black/gold paper (Shizen)
Gold corrugated paper (Shizen)
Gold ribbon, $\frac{1}{4}$" wide
Craft glue

1. Use the top of the bubbles as a template to cut the black/gold paper. Glue it to the top.

2. Cut the corrugated paper $\frac{1}{4}$" x 4". Glue around the rim and trim where the ends meet.

3. Cut the tissue 2" x $3\frac{1}{2}$". Wrap around the bottle and tape on the bottom and sides to secure.

4. Wrap the gold ribbon around the neck of the bottle and tie into a bow.

Pattern for Harlequin
Shower Invitation (pg 56)

Pattern for Black Toile
Shower Invitation (pg 22)

Alternate heart patterns

Should you make your own invitations?

1. Do you have enough time before the wedding?

2. Can you elicit help from friends and family?

3. Do you want a really original and unique invitation?

4. Is your wedding budget less than you would hope?

If you answered yes to the above questions, then by-all-means make your own one-of-a kind invitations.

Here are some tips to help you:

Make a sample card first to get a feel for the amount of time and the steps that will be involved. You might want to simplify your design at this point if it seems too complicated. Then:

1. Do all of your cutting at one time.

2. Set up each element in an assembly line.

3. Make assignments to your helpers so that they are only doing one step, for instance, one person ties all the bows, one does all the gluing of papers together, etc.

4. If you're making over fifty invitations, you might ask your local printer for help. Have them cut your paper all at one time in their guillotine cutter (they'll know what this is).

5. Or have them print the invitation information, cut to your specified size. Then you'll just have to add your own unique finishing touches.

joan
smith

megan
alex

Diamonds truly are
a girl's best friend. Here
pastel diamonds of humble
paper adorn fun and informal
wedding items. The colorful adhesive-
backed squares make crafting these cards
easy as can be. The wedding invitation, place
card, and favor box all feature the pastel
diamonds. The bubbles are embellished with
narrow strips of pastel stickers and topped
with a symbolic rhinestone.

Invitation

You'll need:
White paper
White cardstock
1" adhesive-backed vellum squares of lavender, pink, yellow and green (Mrs. Grossman's)
Adhesive-backed vellum strip, green (Mrs. Grossman's)
Two tags, one round lavender, one square yellow
Alphabet stamps (Rubber Stampede)
Bride and Groom stamp #J118 (Stampendous)
Black ink pad
Hole punch (square punch, optional)
Glue stick
Glitter

1. Print the invitation on white paper. Cut 4" x 6".

2. Cut the white cardstock 7" x 10". Score and fold in half. Glue the invitation on the inside.

3. Adhere the colored squares to the left side of the card as pictured. Adhere the green strip along the side of the squares.

4. Stamp the yellow tag with the "bride and groom" design. Stamp the names of the bride and groom on the lavender tag.

5. Punch a hole in the top part of the card and thread the tag strings through. Trim and secure on the back with invisible tape.

6. Optional: Use a glue stick to add glitter to the edge of the bride and groom tag.

Favor Box

You'll need:
White box 3"
1" adhesive-backed vellum square, yellow (Mrs. Grossman's)
White cardstock
Bride and groom stamp #J118 (Stampendous)
Black ink pad
Glue stick
Glitter
10" pink sheer ribbon, $1\frac{1}{2}$" wide

1. Apply the yellow square to a piece of cardstock and cut to $1\frac{1}{2}$" square. Stamp the "bride and groom" design on the yellow square. Rub over the edges of the square with a glue stick and dust with glitter.

2. Fill the box with truffles or other candies.

3. Wrap the ribbon around the box and glue on the bottom.

4. Glue the stamped square over the top of the ribbon.

Make it Easy

The square stickers used on these projects are so easy to use. They can decorate other items such as number and menu cards and thank you notes, too. Just apply the stickers and stamp. What could be easier?

Place Card

You'll need:
White cardstock
1" adhesive-backed square, pink (Mrs. Grossman's)
Alphabet stamps (Rubber Stampede)
Bride and Groom stamp #J118 (Stampendous)
Black ink pad
Glue stick
Glitter

1. Cut the white cardstock $3\frac{1}{2}$" x 4". Score and fold in half.

2. Stamp the guest's name on the card.

3. Apply the square to the left hand side of the card on the diagonal. Stamp the "bride and groom" design on the square. Rub over the edges of the square with a glue stick and dust with glitter.

Bubbles

You'll need:
Bottle of bubbles
Purple vellum #61068 (Memories in the Making)
Green, pink, lavender adhesive strips (Mrs. Grossman's)
Adhesive-back rhinestone

1. Cut $\frac{1}{2}$" square of purple vellum and glue to top of the bottle.
2. Adhere the rhinestone to the center of the square.
3. Wrap the adhesive strips around the bottle and one around the rim.

Ten Minute Invitations

Accents in Lace

You'll need:
Round paper doily 6"
Yellow floral paper #AG099 (Anna Griffin)
Dark yellow floral paper #AG041 (Anna Griffin)
Glue stick
Font: Edwardian Script

1. Cut the dark yellow floral paper to a size that will easily go through your printer. Print the invitation, then cut the paper to $3\frac{1}{2}$" x 7".

2. Cut the lighter yellow paper 6" x 8". Glue the invitation sheet in the center of this sheet using a glue stick.

3. Cut the round doily in half. Glue one half to the top along the top edge of the card and again at the bottom along the bottom edge using a glue stick.

Rose Petals

You'll need:
Ivory card, 5" x $6\frac{5}{8}$" with $2\frac{1}{2}$" x 4"
  rectangular opening
Ivory tulle
Red silk rose petals
$\frac{1}{2}$ yd. ivory feather-edged ribbon
Glue stick
Craft glue

1. Print the invitation on a piece of ivory paper. Cut to $4\frac{1}{2}$" x 6" and glue to the inside of the card.

2. Cut the tulle to 5" x 8".

3. Open the card and put a line of craft glue all around the opening about $\frac{1}{2}$" from the edge.

4. Lay half of the tulle over the opening and into the glue. The other half should extend beyond.

5. Lay the petals on the tulle in the opening area. Fold up the tulle and press into the still wet glue. Allow to dry before closing and tie the ribbon around and into a bow.

6. Optional: Instead of gluing, sew the tulle into bags.

We know how many things you'll need to do before your wedding. So we've designed some cards that are quick to make. These six invitations can be made in a flash. Use combinations of the same papers and ribbons to create place cards, menu cards, programs, and more.

Golden Threads

You'll need:
Gold embroidered paper (Shizen)
Ivory paper
16 gold metallic ribbon, $1\frac{1}{2}$" wide
Glue stick
Font: Edwardian Script

1. Print the invitation on ivory paper. Cut to $4\frac{1}{2}$" x 6".

2. Print "You're Invited" on ivory paper and cut to 1" x 3".

3. Cut the embroidered paper to 7" x 11" rounding the corners slightly. Glue the invitation to the inside of the card using a glue stick.

4. Fold the card and glue the "You're Invited" strip to the front of the card $2\frac{1}{2}$" from the top and centered.

5. Wrap the gold ribbon around the card and tie in a bow on the right hand side. Glue in various spots to secure.

Isn't It Romantic

You'll need:
Pink floral paper #AG125 (Anna Griffin)
Pink stripe paper (Color Bok)
16" pink sheer ribbon, 1" wide
Glue stick
Font: Edwardian Script

1. Print invitation on the pink stripe paper and cut to 6" x 7".

2. Cut the floral paper to 7" x 12". With a compass mark half circles on each short edge of the paper. Cut the half rounds using a craft knife.

3. Glue the invitation to the inside center of the card. Score, then fold each half circle into the center of the card. Punch a hole in the center edge of each half circle.

4. Thread the ribbon through the holes from the back and tie into a bow on the front.

Something Blue

You'll need:
Aqua floral #AG056 (Anna Griffin)
White cardstock
White wedding flowers with pearls
Glue gun
Font: Edwardian Script

1. Print the invitation on white paper. Cut to $3\frac{1}{2}$" x 6".

2. Cut the aqua floral paper to 5" x 7".

3. Glue the invitation in the center of the floral paper.

4. Hot glue the white flowers and pearls to the upper left corner of the invitation and one flower to the lower right corner.

Golden Leaves

You'll need:
Brown floral paper #AG110 (Anna Griffin)
Ivory cardstock
3 natural skeleton leaves (2 large, 1 small)
Glue stick
Craft glue
Font: Edwardian Script

1. Print the invitation on the ivory paper. Cut to $3\frac{3}{4}$" x $5\frac{3}{4}$".

2. Cut the brown floral paper to $5\frac{1}{2}$" x 7".

3. With a glue stick, glue the invitation in the center of the floral paper.

4. With tiny dots of craft glue, glue two large skeleton leaves to the lower left corner and the small leaf to the upper right corner.

Showers

This collection of dots and stripes will surely appeal to a free-spirited hostess. Her artistically layered invitation will certainly garner everyone's attention. Darling little striped favor boxes are decoration enough when displayed together on a table or shelf. Shower memories are kept alive in the pages of this clever booklet designed to keep track of gifts, write shower anecdotes and maybe include some candid photos.

You're Invited

TIME
DATE
PLACE
FOR

Shower Memories

Dots and Stripes

Shower Memory Book

You'll need:
Ivory cardstock
Lime/yellow stripe paper #61069
  (Memories in the Making)
Blue/lime stripe paper #61070
  (Memories in the Making)
Blue/yellow/green dot paper #61076
  (Memories in the Making)
Yellow solid paper #61086
  (Memories in the Making)
16" green/white polka dot ribbon, $1\frac{1}{2}$" wide
Glue stick
Font: Edwardian Script

1. Cut the ivory cardstock $8\frac{1}{2}$" x 11".

2. Cut solid yellow paper $8\frac{1}{2}$" x 11". Glue to the ivory cardstock using a glue stick. Score and fold in half.

3. Cut a strip of blue/yellow/green dot paper 4" x $8\frac{1}{2}$". Glue this strip to the left side of the yellow paper.

4. Cut the lime/yellow stripe paper 6" x $8\frac{1}{2}$". Fold in half lengthwise and place over the fold on the card. Glue in place.

5. Cut the blue/lime stripe paper $2\frac{3}{4}$" x 11". Glue horizontally on the card and around to the back (refer to photo for placement).

6. Print "Shower Memories" on yellow paper. Cut paper $1\frac{3}{4}$" x $4\frac{1}{4}$". Glue in the center of the blue/lime stripe paper.

7. Open up the card. Score and fold several sheets of $8\frac{1}{2}$" x 11" pieces of blank paper. Place inside of the card. Punch two holes through the papers and the card on the fold.

8. Thread a ribbon through the holes from the inside and tie into a knot. Trim the tails.

(This booklet can be used to record gifts, used as a guest book, to jot down funny things that happen at the shower, list games played, list the winners, display shower photographs, etc.)

Shower Invitation

You'll need:
Ivory cardstock
Lime/yellow stripe paper #61069
  (Memories in the Making)
Pink/lime stripe paper #61065
  (Memories in the Making)
Blue/lime stripe paper #61070
  (Memories in the Making)
Blue/lime/yellow dots #61076
  (Memories in the Making)
"You're Invited" stamp, #F993 (Hero Arts)
Black ink pad
Yellow envelope
Craft glue

1. Cut the paper as follows:
  ivory cardstock 4" x $5\frac{1}{2}$"
  blue/lime stripe 4" x $5\frac{1}{2}$"
  pink/lime stripe $3\frac{1}{4}$" x $5\frac{3}{4}$"
  blue/lime/yellow dot 3" x $4\frac{1}{2}$"
  lime/yellow stripe $2\frac{1}{2}$" x $3\frac{1}{4}$"

2. Glue the blue/lime stripe paper to the ivory cardstock.

3. Center and glue the papers as in the photograph.

4. Stamp the "Invitation" information in the center of the card (or copy from page 71).

Favor Boxes

You'll need:
Lime/yellow stripe #61176 (Memories in Making)
Pink/lime stripe #61065 (Memories in Making)
Blue/lime stripe #61064 (Memories in Making)
Pink/yellow stripe #61074 (Memories in Making)
Victorian alphabet stickers #64168
  (Memories in the Making)

1. Trace and cut out the pattern on pages 78 & 79.

2. Use the pattern to cut out the favor boxes from assorted papers. Score and fold the paper and form the box (see photo).

3. Apply an initial sticker (of the honored guest's first name) to the round areas.

You're invited

Marie

Unexpected details can make all the difference. This shower ensemble combines a variety of design elements from polka dots, to ticking, swirls and checks. The invitation is neatly stamped and bordered in cheerful dots. The crisp white doily holds a paper napkin too pretty to use. The place card sports a checkerboard bow as does the thank you card.

Red Letter Day

Invitation

You'll need:
White embossed card (The Write Stock) $3\frac{1}{2}$" x 5"
 or white cardstock
Red/white dot paper #61014
 (Memories in the Making)
"You're Invited" stamp #B8175
 (Calif. Rubber Stamp Co.)
Black ink pad
Craft knife
Glue stick
Glue gun

1. Cut two strips of red dot paper $\frac{3}{8}$" x 5" and two $\frac{3}{8}$" x $3\frac{1}{2}$".
2. Apply glue stick along the edge of the card and adhere the strips one at a time overlapping at each corner. Quickly, before the glue dries, cut a diagonal cut at each corner through both strips of paper. Remove the cuttings at each corner. This will miter the corners neatly.
3. Stamp "You're Invited" in the middle of the card.
4. Add a bow to the upper left hand corner.

Thank You Note

You'll need:
White embossed card (The Write Stock), 5" x 7"
 or white cardstock
Red/white dot #61014 (Memories in the Making)
Red/white ticking #61006 (Memories in Making)
Red/white spiral #61154 (Memories in Making)
16" red/white check ribbon, $\frac{1}{2}$" wide (May Arts)
Craft glue
Glue stick

1. Cut red dot paper $2\frac{1}{2}$" square, red striped paper 2" square, red swirl paper $1\frac{1}{2}$" square.
2. Glue the red dot paper on the diagonal so that it forms a diamond shape, then glue the striped paper on straight and the swirl paper on the diagonal.
3. Tie a bow and glue it to the center.

Napkin Holder

You'll need:
White round paper lace doily, 6"
Red/white check paper napkins
Craft glue

1. Fan fold the napkin.
2. Wrap the doily around it and apply a dot of glue to secure.

Place Cards

You'll need:
Purchased place cards with embossed border,
 2" x $3\frac{1}{4}$"
Red/white ticking #61006 (Memories in Making)
10" red/white check ribbon, $\frac{1}{2}$" wide (May Arts)
Craft glue
Calligraphy pen

1. Cut the ticking paper 1" x $2\frac{1}{2}$". Write names between the stripes using a calligraphy pen.
2. Adhere the paper to the bottom part of the embossed area of the card. (If desired, you can use white cardstock cut to 4" x 4" folded in half).
3. Tie a bow and glue it to the center top.

More Shower Ideas

This red and white shower was derived from the new bride's kitchen colors. The rest of the shower decorations and flowers carried through this theme, right to the refreshments which were strawberry shortcake and strawberry punch.

It's fun to develop your own shower ideas using the new bride's decorating color schemes or her special interests. Other ideas might be a linen shower, personal or lingerie, hours of the day, rooms of the house, or recipe shower in which the guests provide a special recipe along with the ingredients or tools.

This creamy ivory set is composed of muted hues and sepia tones that are reminiscent of vintage ephemera. The calligraphy paper edges the invitation and tops the favor box. The luscious floral paper adds a lovely texture to both. A lone butterfly delicately decorates each item including the place card.

Butterfly Garden

Shower Invitation

You'll need:
Brown floral paper #AG107 (Anna Griffin)
Word Sepia #61225 (Memories in the Making)
Butterfly sticker #64189 (Memories in the Making)
$4\frac{1}{2}$" black/white check ribbon, $\frac{1}{2}$" wide
"You're Invited" stamp #B8175
   (Calif. Rubber Stamp Co.)
Black ink pad
Craft glue
Glue stick

1. Cut the ivory cardstock 6" x 9".

2. Cut the brown floral paper 6" x 9" and glue to the cardstock. Score and fold in half.

3. Cut the "Word Sepia" paper to $2\frac{1}{4}$" x $4\frac{1}{2}$" and glue to the left side of the front of the card.

4. Glue the ribbon over the seam using craft glue.

5. Affix the butterfly sticker over the ribbon.

6. Stamp "You're Invited" to the lower right portion of the card.

Place Card

You'll need:
Ivory cardstock
Butterfly sticker #64189 (Memories in the Making)
2" black/white check ribbon, $\frac{1}{2}$" wide
Brown calligraphy pen
Craft glue
Glue stick

1. Cut the ivory cardstock $2\frac{1}{2}$" x 4". Score and fold in half.

2. Glue the ribbon to the left side of the card using craft glue.

3. Affix the butterfly sticker over the top of the ribbon.

4. Write guest's name using the brown calligraphy pen.

Favor

You'll need:
3" round papier mache box
Word Sepia paper #61225 (Memories in Making)
Brown floral paper #AG107 (Anna Griffin)
Butterfly sticker #64189 (Memories in the Making)
12" black/white check ribbon, $\frac{1}{4}$" wide
Glue stick

1. Cut the brown floral paper to fit the side of the box and adhere using a glue stick.

2. Use the top of the box as a template to trace a circles on the back of the "Word Sepia" paper. Cut and glue to the top of the box.

3. Glue the ribbon around the rim of the top of the box.

4. Affix the butterfly sticker to the top center of the box.

You're Invited

To a Wedding Shower

For:

Time:

Date:

Place:

Given by:

(May be copied for personal use)

It's a Shower

For:

Time:

Date:

Place:

Given by:

Spring

You'll need:
Ivory cardstock
Ivory paper
Lavender mulberry paper (Shizen)
Glassine envelope $2\frac{1}{4}$" x $3\frac{1}{2}$"
2 to 3 lavender silk flowers
4" variegated lavender ribbon, $1\frac{1}{2}$" wide
Glue stick
Lavender wired thread (May Arts)
Font: Edwardian Script

1. Cut the ivory cardstock $5\frac{1}{2}$" x $8\frac{1}{2}$". Score and fold in half.

2. Print the invitation and "You're Invited" on ivory paper. Cut the invitation $3\frac{1}{2}$" x 4" and the "You're Invited" $\frac{1}{2}$" x $2\frac{1}{4}$".

3. Glue the invitation to the inside of the card.

4. Tear the mulberry paper to 3" x $4\frac{1}{2}$". Glue to the center of the card.

5. Glue the "You're Invited" strip to the center of the glassine envelope.

6. Insert two to three lavender flowers in the envelope.

7. Place the envelope in the center of the card and glue the flap down to the card. Use a hole punch to make two holes in the top left corner of the envelope and through the front of the card.

8. Thread the ribbon through the two holes from the back to the front of the card and tie in a knot. Notch the ends of the ribbon. Tie the wired thread around the knot and curl the ends.

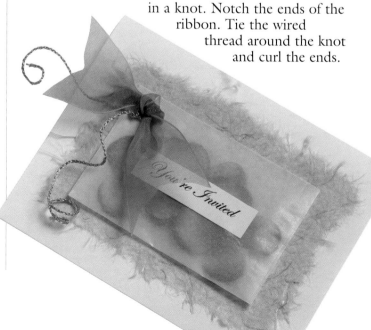

Winter

You'll need:
Forest green cardstock
Burgundy mulberry paper (Shizen)
Ivory paper
Glassine envelope 2" x $3\frac{1}{2}$"
Four gold photo corners
Deckle edge scissors
Glue stick
Glitter
White dried flowers with glitter
Font: Edwardian Script

1. Cut the green cardstock $5\frac{1}{2}$" x $8\frac{1}{2}$". Score and fold in half.

2. Print the invitation on the desired color of paper. Cut 4" x 5". Glue to the inside of the card.

3. Cut the burgundy paper $3\frac{1}{2}$" x $4\frac{1}{2}$" and glue to the center of the green card.

4. Print "You're Invited" on ivory paper and cut into a $1\frac{1}{4}$" x 2" oval using deckle edge scissors. Glue glitter around the edges of the oval.

5. Glue the glittered oval to the center of the glassine envelope.

6. Place the dried flowers in the envelope and the gold photo corners on each corner and glue to the center of the burgundy paper.

When choosing your theme, you might consider one that goes with the time of year of your wedding. The following are examples of invitations for each season.

Summer

You'll need:
Ivory paper
Textured handmade ivory paper
16" green corrugated strip, $\frac{1}{2}$" wide (Loose Ends)
Glassine envelope 2" x 3$\frac{1}{2}$"
Silk sunflower
Glue stick
Craft knife
8" yellow and gold stripe ribbon, $\frac{1}{2}$" wide

1. Print the invitation on ivory paper. Cut 4" x 5".

2. Cut the handmade paper 6" x 10". Score and fold in half. Glue the invitation on the inside of the card.

3. Insert the sunflower in the glassine envelope. Place the envelope in the center front of the card and punch two holes in the top and through the front of the card. Thread the ribbon through these holes from the back to the front and tie into a bow.

4. Glue the corrugated strips to border the envelope, mitering the corners.

Fall

You'll need:
Kraft card
  stock
Ivory paper
Ivory cardstock
Corrugated
  paper
"you're invited"
  stamp #B8175
  (Calif. Rubber
  Stamp Co.)
Autumn Tree stamp
  #LL607 Nature's
Silhouettes Set (Hero
  Arts)
Deckle edge scissors
Glue stick
Craft knife
Brown ink pad
Glassine envelope 2$\frac{1}{4}$" x 3$\frac{1}{2}$"
Twine
Leaf

1. Cut kraft cardstock 6" x 8". Score and fold in half.

2. Print the invitation on ivory paper. Cut 4" x 6" and glue to the inside of the kraft card.

3. Cut one piece of ivory cardstock 2$\frac{1}{4}$" square and another one 3$\frac{1}{2}$" x 4$\frac{1}{2}$" using deckle edge scissors.

4. Stamp the autumn tree design on the 2$\frac{1}{4}$" square. Stamp "you're invited" on ivory cardstock. Using a craft knife, cut to $\frac{3}{4}$" x 3$\frac{1}{4}$" and cut the bottom edge of the stamped strip, cutting around the "y" (refer to photograph).

5. Cut the corrugated paper 3" x 4" and glue the "you're invited" strip around the bottom edge as in the photograph.

6. Triple layer these pieces to the kraft card using a glue stick.

7. Insert a leaf in the glassine envelope. Punch a hole in the corner of the envelope and the top front edge of the card. Tie the envelope to the card through the hole using twine. Tie in a knot and trim tails.

Reflections

You'll need:

Ivory dot cardstock (Lasting Impressions for Paper)
Peach paper
Blue floral paper (Anna Griffin)
Beige skeleton leaf
Self-adhesive flat bottom marble (Bits and Baubles by Creative Imaginations)
Vintage wedding photo ("Marry Me" by Art Chix Studio) or a photo copy of the couple
Glue stick
Craft glue

1. Cut ivory cardstock 5" x 7". Score and fold in half.

2. Cut the blue floral paper $2\frac{1}{4}$" square with the deckle edge scissors. Cut the peach paper $1\frac{1}{2}$" square.

3. Apply the marble to the photo and trim around the edge.

4. Glue the two papers together and glue on the marble/photo. Glue this layered piece to the card.

5. Add a small amount of craft glue to the back of the leaf and glue as shown in the photo.

6. Handwrite, print or stamp the invitation on the inside.

This could be used for either a shower or a wedding invitation.

Picture Perfect

You'll need:

Purchased kraft card, 7" x 10" or kraft cardstock
Ivory paper
Newsprint paper #61098 (Memories in the Making)
Brown floral paper #AG107 (Anna Griffin)
Calligraphy photo mount #0985 (Design Originals)
Photograph copies
Glue stick
Font: Edwardian Script

1. Print "You're Invited" on ivory paper. If you don't have a computer, you can use a rubber stamp with the same wording. Cut the printed ivory paper to $\frac{3}{4}$" x $3\frac{1}{2}$".

2. Have several copies of the guest of honor's photo made at a print shop. Cut these copies to 1" x $1\frac{1}{2}$". Glue the photos on the back of the photo mount using a glue stick.

3. Cut the brown floral paper to $2\frac{3}{4}$" x $3\frac{1}{2}$" and the newsprint paper to $3\frac{1}{2}$" x 4". Layer these pieces and glue using a glue stick.

4. Fold the kraft card in half and glue the layered pieces to the front of the card $\frac{3}{4}$" from the top. Glue the "You're Invited" strip to the lower portion of the card 1" up from the bottom.

Groomsmen's Thank You Card

You'll need:
Ivory cardstock
Oxfordchalk Graphite paper #61028
  (Memories in the Making)
Houndstooth Taupe paper #61022
  (Memories in the Making)
Stamp – "Thanks" #5702F (Inky Antics)
Black ink pad

1. Fold the 7" x 10" ivory cardstock in half.

2. Cut the grey stripe paper 4" x 6" and the Houndstooth paper, 3" x 5".

3. Stamp "Thanks" to the center of the striped paper using a black ink pad.

4. Glue the striped paper to the center of the houndstooth, and then both to the center of the ivory card.

5. Handwrite the note on the inside.

Floral Portrait

You'll need:
Ivory cardstock
Purple mulberry (Shizen)
Nature Frames sticker #66059
  (Memories in the Making)
8" gold ribbon, $\frac{5}{8}$" wide
Craft glue

1. Cut ivory cardstock 7" x 10". Score and fold in half.

2. Tear the mulberry paper into a $2\frac{1}{2}$" x 7" strip and glue to the front of the card (see page 39).

3. Wrap the ribbon all the way around the front panel of the card starting on the inside and ending on the front. Trim the ends of the ribbon where they meet. Don't overlap.

4. Press the floral sticker to the center of the card.

5. Print the invitation on a separate piece of paper and glue to the inside.

This could be used for either a shower or a wedding invitation.

Gallery of Ideas

Save the Date

You'll need:
Corrugated cards 4" x 5" (Paper Reflections)
Envelope
Ivory paper
"Postal Pieces" stickers (Stickopotamus,
 EK Success)
Glue stick
Font: Times

1. Print the wedding information on ivory paper. Cut to fit the inside of the card, approximately 3" x 4" and glue to the inside of the card using a glue stick.

2. Print "Save the Date" on ivory paper and cut to $\frac{1}{2}$" to $2\frac{1}{2}$". Glue to the front of the card about $1\frac{3}{4}$" from the top.

3. Use the stickers to decorate the card, the calendar at the bottom and the stamps scattered.

4. Use one of the cancelled stamp stickers to seal the envelope.

Initial Offering

You'll need:
Ivory cardstock
Ivory paper
Burgundy print #AG002 (Anna Griffin)
Brown floral #AG107 (Anna Griffin)
Brown solid paper
"B" Initial, alphabet set #2480P (Anna Griffin)
Black ink pad
8" ivory sheer ribbon with stripe, $\frac{5}{8}$" wide
Black photo corners
Glue stick
Craft glue

1. Cut the ivory cardstock $5\frac{1}{2}$" x 8".

2. Score 2" in from each short end. Fold in to the middle to form doors.

3. Cut the brown floral paper $2\frac{1}{4}$" square, the red floral $1\frac{3}{4}$" square, the brown solid $1\frac{1}{2}$" square.

4. Stamp the initial in the center of the brown paper. Place the photo corners on each corner. Place on the burgundy square and moisten to hold the corners in place.

5. Glue this to the brown floral paper.

6. Glue the ribbon to the center back of the layered papers. Use a light layer of craft glue and let the ribbon extend 4" on the right side and $1\frac{3}{4}$" on the left side.

7. Glue the layered square to the left fold of the card.

8. Handwrite or use a computer to write the invitation on a piece of ivory paper. Cut slightly less than 4" x $5\frac{1}{2}$" and glue to the inside.

9. Wrap the ribbon around and tie on the right side.

CD Covers

Name That Tune

You'll need:

Ivory cardstock
Music stamp #141J
 (All Night Media)
"A" stamp B2013
 (Stamparosa)

Border Stamp
 #3192D (Rubber
 Stampede)
Gold ink pad
Blue ink pad
Velcro® dots
Scallop edge scissors

Love's Sweet Songs
(see page 50
for instructions)

Name
That Tune

1. Cut ivory cardstock 7" x 11".
2. Mark and score 1" on each long side, $2\frac{1}{4}$"
from the top and $3\frac{1}{2}$" from the bottom.
3. Stamp the top $2\frac{1}{4}$" area with the music stamp and gold ink.
4. Cut the top edge with scallop edge scissors.
5. Fold in and glue the two 1" sides. Fold up the bottom
edge and glue along the sides to form the pocket.
6. Fold down the top flap.
7. Stamp a piece of ivory paper with the border stamp and
blue ink. Stamp the initial in the center using blue ink.
8. Adhere half the image to the center of the flap with the
glue stick.
9. Glue the Velcro® dots to the inside edge of the flap and
front of folder.

Rosebud Rhapsodies

You'll need:

Textured handmade
 paper (Shizen)
Ivory Bagasse (Shizen)
Rosebud (Shizen)
Fuchsia cardstock
Ivory paper

1 yd. fuchsia silk ribbon, $\frac{1}{4}$" wide
Hole punch
Large eyed, sharp needle
Glue stick
Velcro® dots
Font: Edwardian Script

1. Print the message on the ivory paper.
2. Cut the messages into $1\frac{1}{2}$" x $3\frac{1}{2}$" pieces, the fuchsia
cardstock 2" x 4" and the rosebud paper $2\frac{3}{4}$" x $4\frac{1}{2}$".
Triple layer these pieces using a glue stick.
3. Cut the textured paper $5\frac{1}{2}$" x 6" and the Bagasse paper
6" x 9".
4. Fold the Bagasse paper down $3\frac{1}{2}$" forming the flap for the
CD holder.
5. Place the textured paper on the bagasse paper so that the
bottom edges match. Punch holes through both layers of paper
around all edges about $\frac{3}{4}$" apart using a small hole punch.
6. Thread the needle with the silk ribbon and sew the two papers
together through the punched holes. Trim the ribbon on the back
neatly and glue to adhere.
7. Glue the layered piece to the flap. Insert your CD. Close with
Velcro® dots if desired.

Rosebud
Rhapsodies

A selection of our favorite music
Megan and Alex
June 15, 2004

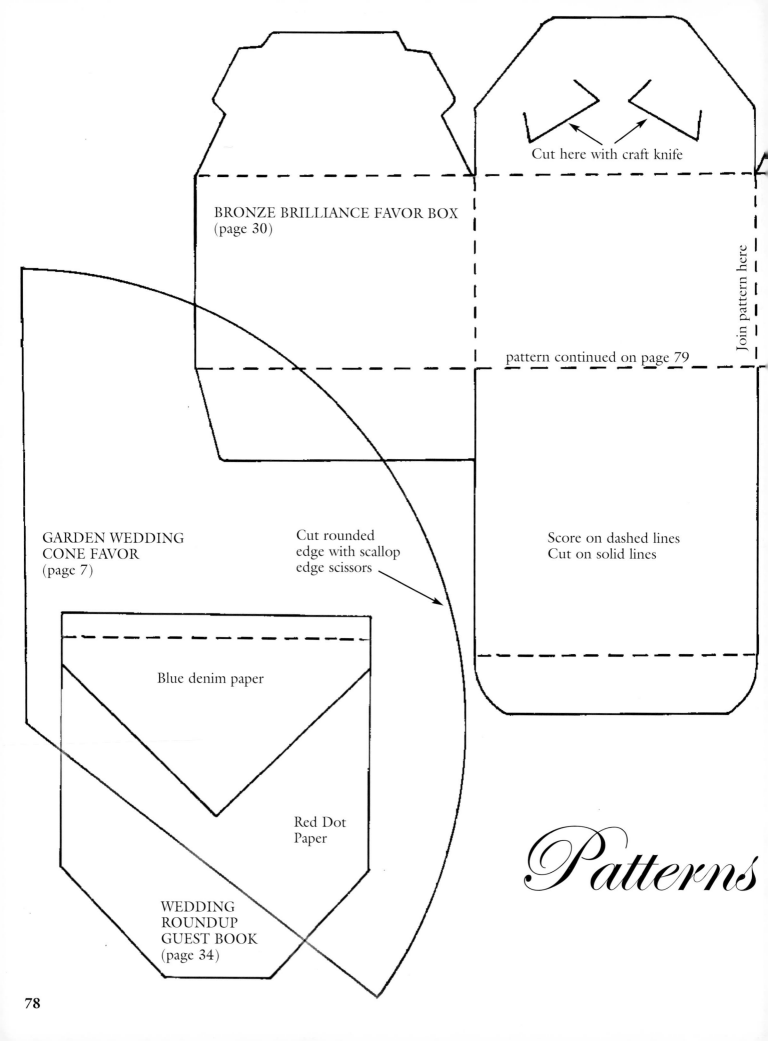

Cut here with craft knife

Join pattern here

BRONZE BRILLIANCE FAVOR BOX
(page 30)

pattern continued on page 79

GARDEN WEDDING
CONE FAVOR
(page 7)

Cut rounded
edge with scallop
edge scissors

Score on dashed lines
Cut on solid lines

Blue denim paper

Red Dot
Paper

WEDDING
ROUNDUP
GUEST BOOK
(page 34)

Patterns

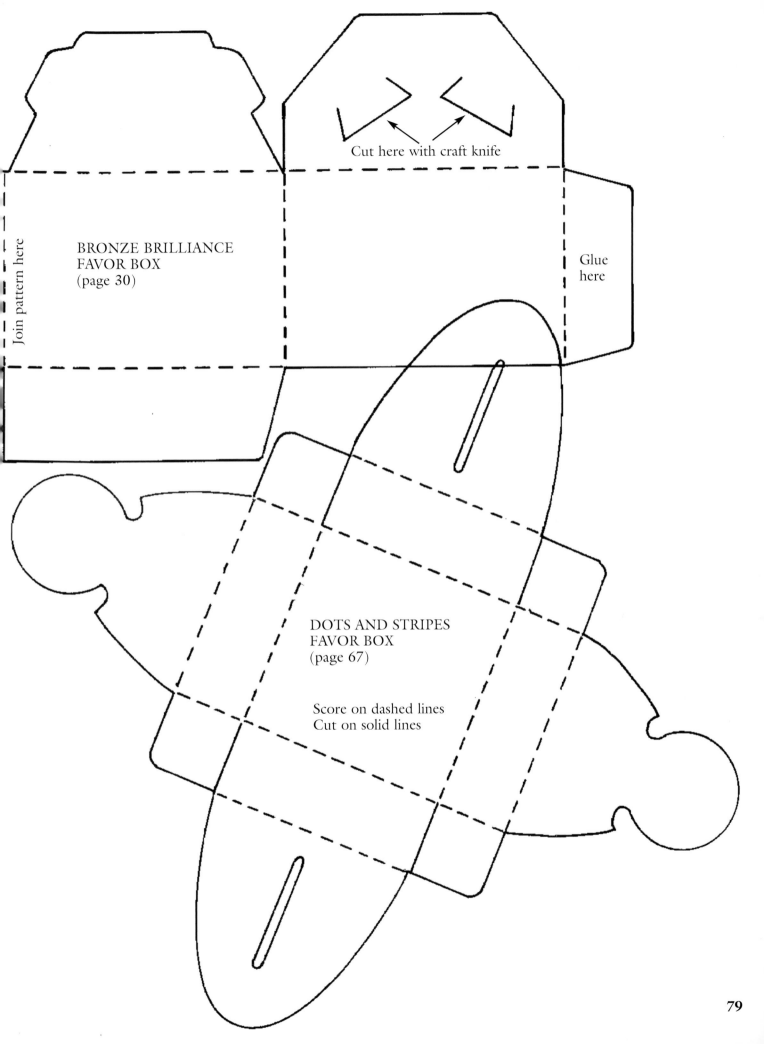

Join pattern here

BRONZE BRILLIANCE
FAVOR BOX
(page 30)

Cut here with craft knife

Glue
here

DOTS AND STRIPES
FAVOR BOX
(page 67)

Score on dashed lines
Cut on solid lines

Invitation Facts

When to send invitations:
Showers
2 to 3 weeks prior to the shower
Save the Date
3 months prior to the wedding
Wedding
4 to 6 weeks prior to the wedding

Wording
There are so many variations on how a wedding invitation is worded. The traditional invitation follows all the rules as shown in the two invitations below. Couples may opt to break the rules so that they can have an invitation which more express their personality. The best way to choose your wording is to visit a stationery store that contains notebooks full of invitation samples. You'll find a wide variety of styles and wording. Talk to the stationer to get ideas on the different variations before you decide to do your own invitations. Take notes and then proceed to design your invitations with the wording that you've chosen. Or consult the internet under "wedding invitations" for other ideas.

The traditional way to word a wedding invitation
Formal for a church wedding:

Mr. and Mrs. Gilbert Jack Brown
request the honour of your presence
at the marriage of their daughter

Elizabeth Ann
to
Mr. Glenn Matthew Smith

Saturday, the tenth of July
Two thousand and four
at two o'clock
Saint Peter's Catholic Church
1554 Stagecoach Drive
Del Mar, California

Formal for a wedding held in other than a church:

Mr. and Mrs. Gilbert Jack Brown
request the pleasure of your company
at the marriage of their daughter

Elizabeth Ann
to
Mr. William Arthur Grant

Saturday, the tenth of June
at two o'clock
in the garden
2627 Via Oeste Lane
Chicago, Illinois

(Note that when it's a church wedding "the honour of your presence" is used. When the wedding will be held in other than a church "request the pleasure of your company" is used.)

Invitation issued by the bride and groom:

The honour of your presence is
requested at
the marriage of

Miss Jerilyn Margaret Eckert
to
Mr. Charles Farrell Clements
etc.
or
Miss Jerilyn Margaret Eckert
and
Mr. Charles Farrell Clements
request the honour of your presence
at their marriage
etc.

If mother uses her maiden name:

Arleen Mae Reis
and Paul William Brown
request the honour of your presence
at the marriage of their daughter

Megan Tosca
to
Mr. Daniel Lyle White
etc.

If mother and father are divorced but have the same name:

Mr. and Mrs. Paul William Brown
request the honour of your presence
at the marriage of their daughter
etc.

If mother and father are divorced but mother has a different name (don't use "and" between their names):

Arleen Mae Reis
Paul William Brown
request the honour of your presence
at the marriage of their daughter

Megan Tosca
to
Mr. Daniel Lyle White

There are many more variations. If you're concerned about the traditional way of wording an invitation, visit your local library or bookstore for books on the subject or consult the internet.